GALETTE!

GALETTE!

Sweet and Savory Recipes as Easy as Pie

REBECCA FIRKSER

Photographs by Jessica Marx

ARTISAN | NEW YORK

Library of Congress Cataloging-in-Publication Data

Names: Firkser, Rebecca, author. | Marx, Jessica, photographer.
Title: Galette! : sweet and savory recipes as easy as pie / Rebecca Firkser;
photographs by Jessica Marx.
Description: New York, NY : Artisan, [2025] | Includes index.
Identifiers: LCCN 2024045355 | ISBN 9781523527069 (hardcover)
Subjects: LCSH: Pies. | Desserts. | LCGFT: Cookbooks.
Classification: LCC TX773 .F568 2025 | DDC 641.86/52—dc23/eng/20241029
LC record available at https://lccn.loc.gov/20

Design by Becky Terhune

Artisan books may be purchased in bulk for business, educational,
or promotional use. For information, please contact your local
bookseller or the Hachette Book Group Special Markets
Department at special.markets@hbgusa.com.

The publisher is not responsible for websites (or their content)
that are not owned by the publisher.

The Hachette Speakers Bureau provides a wide range of authors
for speaking events. To find out more, go to hachettespeakersbureau.com
or email HachetteSpeakers@hbgusa.com.

Published by Artisan,
an imprint of Workman Publishing,
a division of Hachette Book Group, Inc.
1290 Avenue of the Americas
New York, NY 10104
artisanbooks.com

The Artisan name and logo are registered trademarks of Hachette Book Group, Inc.

Printed in China (APO) on responsibly sourced paper
First printing, April 2025

1 3 5 7 9 10 8 6 4 2

For Gail—my mom
(and my first baking teacher)

CONTENTS

"ONE MAKES A PIE [OR GALETTE!] OUT OF ORDINARY STUFF, LIKE RAISINS, SQUASH, OR APPLES AND GIFT WRAPS IT, IN A SENSE, WITH A CRUST. IT'S VERY MAGICAL, VERY SPECIAL."

—WAYNE THIEBAUD

INTRODUCTION

One of the first recipes I developed was a plum galette. I was most of the way through college, swiftly realizing I cared more about cooking than my coursework. I'd started a food blog a couple of years prior and was slowly transitioning from solely making other people's recipes to trusting my own insights. I'd look through cookbooks and online recipes for inspiration, then let my imagination run wild. One warm afternoon, I walked to the tiny grocery store in town and was met with a rare treat: Italian prune plums. An hour's pay from my work-study job got me a few handfuls of fruit and a package of (the cheapest) butter. I hustled the goods back to my little shared kitchen with an idea forming. Carefully, I halved and pitted each plum and tossed them in what I thought might complement the fruit: vanilla extract, orange zest, crunchy sugar. *Would grated ginger be overpowering? I'll add just a bit*, I thought. I timidly rubbed the butter into flour, used a wine bottle to roll out my best approximation of an even round, and tucked the filling into its pastry blanket. As it baked, a crack in the dough swelled, plum juice oozing out and around the crust. The galette was ruined.

Or so I thought! Lo and behold, the bottom turned out crisp, while the fruit baked so soft I could cut it with a spoon. A bite was a symphony of buttery crust and honey-sweet plums, tempered with gingery warmth. I rejoiced.

All these years later, having made food the center of my career, I still think of galettes as an ideal bake for home cooks. The dough, made in advance, offers the opportunity to take your time;

and unlike many baking projects, galette fillings don't necessarily require hyperspecificity when it comes to ingredients. Run out of peaches? Make up the difference with those cherries in the back of your freezer. Toss in extra cinnamon (or what the hell, swap in cardamom if that sounds better). Go ahead and use grapefruit juice when the recipe calls for lemon. It's difficult to mar a galette to the point of inedibility.

Technically speaking, a galette is a flat filled pastry. Dating back in some form to at least the eleventh century, the term's likely origin is *gale*, the Norman dialect of Old French for "flat cake." As culinary history and culture evolved, so too did the galette. Out in the world, you may see the term refer to various regional dishes, from cookies to crepes. When I say "galette," I'm talking about a rustic, typically free-form, pastry with a flaky shortcrust base that's pleated into small folds a couple of inches over the top, leaving the rest of the filling exposed.

Galette pastry is often filled with fruit or vegetables. If you think this sounds like a pie or tart, you're right, sort of. Always baked in some kind of vessel, pies tend to have separate top and bottom crusts; tarts are thinner, open-faced (with raw or baked fillings), and have a crumbly shortcrust, flaky puff pastry, or even an unbaked base. Perhaps you've also seen the term "crostata" used to characterize similar pastries. *Crostata* translates from Italian to "tart," but the product often looks like a galette.

Galettes are made from simple ingredients, with minimal equipment, meaning if your kitchen is stocked with the basics, you can put one together for no more than the cost of fresh (or frozen!) produce. They can be prepared in advance—the raw dough freezes beautifully, and the whole pastry can be baked a full day ahead. They travel well: Bring one right on the sheet pan, or nestle slices into a large ziplock bag or a parchment-lined pizza box. They can be filled with just about any combination of fruit or vegetables (and it doesn't matter one bit if the produce is a tad under- or overripe), as well as meat and cheese that complement each other. They bake up stunningly beautiful, even if assembled haphazardly.

Some of the galettes in this book are extra-large: Like slab pies, they're about the size of a sheet pan, and perfect for big groups. Others are tiny, easy-to-grab snacks that require no plates or even forks. Centerpiece-worthy galettes are baked in a skillet, a fluted tart pan, or a springform cake pan for extra height.

Can you roll out of bed, plop sugared berries or salted tomatoes in a crust with a bit of lemon juice, fold around the edges, and bake a gorgeous galette? *Yes*. And I'll tell you how to do that (see page 132). But we'll have some fun with more creative fillings, too. They will surprise and delight even those weird people in your life who swear they "don't like pastries."

Another item for the galette "pros" column is riffability. Just because you happened upon the Figgy Miso galette (page 110) in the dead of winter, when there is nary a fresh fig to be found, doesn't mean you can't make a tweaked version with sliced apples. Say the market is flooded with zucchini, but someone already got all the eggplant? Swap that summer squash into your Spicy Eggplant Parm galette (page 165).

As you bake through this book, I hope you challenge yourself but aren't an overly harsh critic of your skills. (People who claim to be afraid of making dough: I'm talking to you!) Sometimes, galettes spring a leak. Before you despair, take a good look at that sticky jam pooling around the pastry: It's modern art. Your crust may be a smidge over- or underworked, leading to a slightly dense or crumbly base. But if you follow the filling recipe, eaters will be too busy making yum sounds to notice. Parts of the crust can get a little darker than intended in the oven. But you know what? *Bien cuit* is a French baking term meaning "well done," or deeply caramelized. All of which is to say, simply: **Don't let perfect be the enemy of a good galette.**

READ THIS BEFORE BAKING

The tools and ingredients required to successfully make a galette are few. (There are of course some extras that will make your life easier and your bakes more delicious.) But even if you own none of these, you're in luck: Everything can be sourced from a local store that sells kitchen supplies—you could probably even find all you need at a well-stocked supermarket. Which works out, because you can tackle your grocery list while you're there.

TOOLS

In a pinch, if you have a sheet pan, something to roll with (preferably a rolling pin, but wine or vinegar bottles work great!), and tools for measuring, you can put together a gorgeous galette. Ideally, if you're outfitting your home kitchen for baking, the following are tools I'd recommend investing in. You'll use them over and over—and not just for galettes. In addition, consider having some other inexpensive items that always make your life easier when baking: an **offset spatula** for adept spreading, a **vegetable peeler**, a roll of **masking tape** and a **marker** for labeling prepared elements and leftovers, **aluminum foil** for tenting too-dark portions of crust or filling, a **ruler**, and a few **cotton kitchen towels**.

(See Resources, page 228, for my preferred brands.)

SHEET PAN(S): Whether you call it a cookie sheet, baking sheet, or sheet pan, this tool is a kitchen superhero. Every recipe in this book was developed to be baked on a standard 18-by-13-inch (46 by 33 cm) rimmed half-sheet pan made of sturdy aluminum. It accommodates four tiny galettes and up to one extra-large galette that roughly fills the pan's area. The rim catches drips should the galette leak at all and helps conduct heat to galettes baked in vessels like tart pans or cast-iron skillets (more on those in a minute). If you already own a smaller jelly-roll pan or a flat (unrimmed) cookie sheet, you can of course use it instead, though you'll miss out on some of the advantages of a half-sheet pan. Look for Nordic Ware's Naturals Aluminum Baker's Half Sheet, which is often sold in a two-pack—perfect, as that's also the minimum number of sheet pans I recommend owning.

DIGITAL SCALE: A digital scale is like math: The numbers don't lie. This is extremely helpful in baking, where a change in volume can completely alter a recipe. Learning to measure by weight (in grams and dry ounces or pounds) as opposed to volume (cups, milliliters, and fluid ounces) may take some getting used to, but I personally find the former far easier. It's also exceptionally helpful to weigh your produce before getting too deep into the recipe, as opposed to discovering you're short on something midmeasure. The Escali Primo Digital Food Scale is my favorite. Of course, if you don't want to buy a scale, or are baking in a kitchen that doesn't have one, the recipes in this book include volume measurements.

MEASURING CUPS AND SPOONS: Get dishwasher-safe measuring cups and spoons that stack into one another for tidy storage. And if they're attached by a metal hinged snap ring, do yourself a favor and remove it—storing them in the same place in your kitchen is an equally effective way to avoid losing any, and you won't risk getting the rest dirty when using one.

ROLLING PIN: Rolling pins come in so many sizes, shapes, and materials. Dowel rolling pins, which are single rods (as opposed to the handled versions usually found in American home kitchens), are often preferred by professional bakers and are the easiest to use once you get the hang of them. French dowel pins are tapered at the ends, which allows you to manipulate different pressures at once, helping to evenly roll out cold, firm dough. On the other hand, you might find a straight dowel pin better for getting an even thickness throughout. Foot-long or shorter pins (sometimes known as Chinese or dumpling pins) help you apply controlled, concentrated pressure, which is especially useful for rolling dough into even rounds or rectangles (and of course are handy if you're working with limited counter space). Rolling out crust with a longer pin, especially a tapered one, usually goes more quickly, which is great for large dough slabs. Handled pins, however, can be effective for those with limited hand or wrist mobility. I like different sizes and shapes of pins for different baking projects, but I always prefer a wooden model (not metal, stone, or plastic) about 1½ inches (4 cm) wide and at least 12 inches (30.5 cm) long. Head to a kitchenware store and feel around to see which material, style, length, and thickness you like.

PASTRY BRUSH: You can buy 1-inch (2.5 cm) flat wooden pastry brushes with boar hair bristles from restaurant supply stores for a few dollars, and I don't think you need anything snazzier. They're easy to hand-wash and are the ideal length for brushing egg wash onto galette crust. Silicone brushes are dishwasher-safe and affordable but don't brush as smoothly as bristles. I also often use new paintbrushes from the hardware store—perhaps unorthodox, but they're cheap and work great. (All that said, you *can* use your clean fingers to egg-wash galette crust.)

KNIVES: Any sharp knife will prove a worthy tool for slicing fruit and chopping vegetables. If you're investing in just one, look for a 5-inch (13 cm) petty/prep knife, which is just as useful for slicing

raw apples as for cutting wedges of apple galette.

BENCH OR BOWL SCRAPER: I don't cut butter with a knife; I use a bench scraper for the task. These flat pieces of metal (or plastic) also make easy, efficient work of scooping and transferring ingredients from one surface or vessel to another as well as folding dough together. I like metal bench scrapers (Ateco's are excellent) or a plastic bowl scraper (especially Matfer Bourgeat's), which does all of the above almost as well and is also flexible like a spatula, helpful for removing every last bit of an ingredient from a bowl.

LARGE MIXING BOWL (OR BOWL SET): One large, preferably dishwasher-safe, metal or glass bowl at the very least, and ideally a set of three or more (small, medium, and large options), will be by your side for everything from mixing up your galette crust's dough to tossing together its fillings.

PARCHMENT PAPER OR SILICONE BAKING MATS: Lining a sheet pan with parchment or silicone forms a nonstick landing pad for a galette and catches any leaks that could burn onto the pan. I try to buy compostable parchment to cut back on waste (and silicone mats are washable).

PLASTIC WRAP: For galette dough to properly hydrate, it needs to be wrapped in something airtight and clingy. Plastic wrap is the most widely accessible option. I like Kirkland Stretch-Tite, which is easy to cut and adherent but not overly sticky. I actually reuse plastic wrap for dough—I save it in a container until it's tattered. More sustainable options are gallon-size ziplock bags and W&P's Reusable Stretch Wrap, both of which can be run through the dishwasher. I don't recommend beeswax wraps for pastry dough, as the dough can absorb the waxy flavor.

FOOD PROCESSOR: In the world of galettes, a food processor is only truly necessary when pureeing the nut-based paste known as frangipane, of which there are a few varieties in this book. It also helps those who are short on time or who have limited ability to finely chop produce, or can serve (with the machine's shredding disk) as an alternative to a box grater. And yes, you can use a food processor to make dough for galette crust. I personally sometimes find it more annoying to wash the food processor than a bowl, but it comes in handy when making multiple batches of dough at a time, like at the start of a busy holiday baking season. Further, many people I've polled told me they'd prefer to make dough in the machine and that not having the option might make or break whether they even try a recipe. So there you have it. For the method, see page 31.

BAKING VESSELS: A classic galette is baked free-form, but for some extra height, you can have fun by baking in vessels like springform pans, cast-iron skillets, pie plates, fluted tart pans with removable bottoms, and cake pans.

NOTE: *While it is rare, some glass pie plates and baking dishes (particularly vintage ones) can suffer from shock and shatter when transferred from cold to hot or vice versa. Since the recipes in this book involve freezing a galette before baking it in a hot oven, play it safe by using metal and ceramic vessels.*

PIZZA STONE: For a galette with an extra-crisp bottom and to help keep oven temperatures stable, set a pizza stone in your oven as it preheats. Place the sheet pan with the galette directly on top of the hot pizza stone and bake as directed. Adept bakers can play harder by skipping the sheet pan entirely and starting the galette on a cold, parchment-lined pizza stone or by carefully sliding a galette (on a sheet of parchment) onto a preheated pizza stone. If you're going with the pizza stone—only method, place a sheet pan underneath the oven rack to catch any drips.

SHEET PAN COVERS: Cute as it is to roll up to a picnic with a galette in a pizza box, for taking one on the go, I adore lids that snap perfectly onto sheet pans, much like Tupperware. I own Nordic Ware's version, but there are plenty of options.

LET'S TALK ABOUT OVENS (AND STOVES)

The good news is that any oven, regardless of age, size, or power, is capable of baking off a great galette. The bad news is that each one, as well as the cooktops that often come with them, is different (and even two of the exact same ranges can work differently). The oven's heat source may come from the bottom or the top, which changes how food browns; the heat may circulate powerfully or not so much, affecting cook times, or the oven will be hotter in either the back or the front, meaning you have to rotate your pan to ensure even cooking. And don't even get me started on the differences between gas- and electric-based power.

So much of baking focuses on precision, but because of these variables it's nearly impossible to know what every oven or stove is capable of. While these recipes have been tested in many different kitchens, here's how to ensure success in yours: 1) Buy an oven thermometer, so you can see the temperature reading, as opposed to assuming your oven has reached the temperature it was set to. 2) Pay closer attention to a recipe's visual cues and sensory phrases, like "looks deeply golden" and "smells nutty." As you get comfortable focusing on these indicators—as opposed to minutes and seconds—you'll find that your range's shortcomings matter far less.

INGREDIENTS

If you already bake at home, odds are you have on hand at least some of the following dry and wet ingredients needed to assemble a galette. Luckily, everything below is a staple that will last a long time in your pantry or refrigerator, and is called for in plenty of non-galette recipes. Check out Resources (page 228) for where to find some of these (and more!) ingredients, as well as brand recommendations.

BUTTER: The most important ingredient when it comes to making a rich, flaky galette crust is butter. Unsalted is the way to go, as salted butter's saltiness varies by brand. In the average US supermarket, you're likely to find several brands of American-style butter, and possibly a few European styles; the main difference between them comes down to fat content (see page 33 for more on this). I've tested these recipes with many, many brands of butter, and while I have a few favorites, any will do.

FLOUR: All-purpose flour is my go-to. Bleached or unbleached will work, but save the expensive stone-milled brands for bread (these tend to absorb water differently and are harder to work with in pastry dough).

To explore other types of flour that play nicely with galettes, like **Whole Wheat** and **Buckwheat**, see the Flavored Crust Variations (page 39).

SUGAR: Granulated sugar will get you through all the recipes in this book, with the exception of a few that also call for **brown or powdered (aka confectioners') sugar**. To make light brown sugar from granulated, mix 1 tablespoon molasses into every 1 cup (200 g) granulated sugar; to make powdered sugar, grind granulated sugar in a food processor until it forms a fine powder, then measure out however much you need (1 cup/200 g granulated sugar will make about 1¾ cups/200 g powdered; if making this in advance, you can add 1 tablespoon cornstarch per every 1 cup/200 g sugar to the food processor along with the sugar to prevent caking). Sprinkle extra sugar over the crust of sweet galettes after they're egg-washed for a bit of sparkle and caramelization. I usually just shower over more of the granulated that I used in the filling, but coarse **demerara or turbinado sugar** adds great texture.

SALT: These recipes were developed with **kosher salt**, specifically Diamond Crystal or

Morton kosher salt (the former is half as salty as the latter by volume). Measurements for both appear in the ingredient lists. If you use table or fine sea salt, or even another brand of kosher salt, the amounts will not be the same, so find an equivalent chart or know the risk. For finishing galettes with a bit of texture, I love a sprinkle of **flaky sea salt** (any brand) over the top.

CORNSTARCH: When mixed with liquid and heated, cornstarch acts as a thickener to help prevent galette filling from leaking and/or making the crust soggy. If you don't eat corn, use **arrowroot starch** as a 1:1 swap. **All-purpose flour** can also be used as a cornstarch substitute, but you'll need to double the called-for amount of cornstarch to adequately thicken the filling, which can look cloudy in fruit galettes. (Don't use either substitute in the Almost Cannoli galette, page 117, as you'd need too much flour to properly swap, and arrowroot starch can result in a slimy texture when heated with milk.)

EGGS: You'll use eggs in a few fillings, but for the most part, an egg's job in galette making is to be beaten and brushed onto the exposed crust just before baking. The fatty yolk helps the crust bake deeply golden brown, and the white creates a shiny finish. Egg wash also acts as a glue for adornments like sugar or seeds to adhere to the crust and helps ensure the crust doesn't unfold as it expands in the oven. If you happen to have extra egg whites, you can mimic whole egg wash by beating in heavy cream or milk, 1 tablespoon per 1 egg white.

NOTE: *Each recipe in this book will call for 1 beaten egg to make egg wash, but you won't use all of it for one galette. After applying the egg wash, don't toss the excess—freeze the leftovers in an ice cube tray and thaw a cube for your next galette.*

SPICES AND SEASONINGS: You don't *need* a robust spice cabinet to make a galette, but the following are called for regularly in this book's recipes: **ground cinnamon**, **ground cardamom**, **ground ginger**, **black pepper** (use peppercorns and a grinder as opposed to preground for the best flavor and texture), **fennel seeds**, **cumin** (ground or seeds), **coriander** (ground or seeds), and **red pepper flakes**.

EXTRACTS AND LIQUORS: As with spices, these flavorings will come in handy throughout the recipes in this book, and bonus, they last for years: **vanilla extract**, **almond extract**, **rose water**, and **orange blossom water**. Liquors with a long shelf life, like **bourbon**, **amaro**, **rum**, and **Campari,** are also used in small quantities similar to extracts (but there's always a nonalcoholic option included).

NUTS AND SEEDS: Nuts or seeds are used as the base of frangipane-style galette fillings, as well as to adorn some of the crusts. **Walnuts**, **pecans**, **hazelnuts**, **almonds**, **sesame seeds**, **sunflower seeds**, **pepitas** (a pumpkin seed variety), **almond flour**, and **tahini** (sesame seed paste) grace the pages of this book. Store raw or toasted nuts and seeds in the refrigerator or freezer to keep them fresh for longer.

NOTE: *While you can buy toasted nuts and seeds, the flavor is more robust if you DIY. To toast nuts or seeds: Spread any amount in a single layer on an unlined sheet pan. Bake at 325°F (160°C) until fragrant, 8 to 10 minutes for walnuts, pecans, and pistachios; 10 to 15 minutes for hazelnuts, almonds, pepitas, and sunflower seeds. Let cool completely (if using skin-on hazelnuts, after cooling, rub off their papery brown skins with a towel or your fingers) before incorporating into a recipe.*

HOW TO MEASURE FLOUR

The easiest way to measure flour is to use gram weights. Place a bowl on a digital scale, zero it out in the grams setting, and spoon in the flour until you hit the called-for number (easy!). If using a cup measure, lightly spoon the flour out of its container into the cup—not scooping directly with the cup, not packing the flour into the cup—then level the cup with a straight edge, such as the back of a butter knife or edge of a bench scraper. A common argument among recipe developers is how much 1 cup of flour weighs: It depends on how flour is loaded into a measuring cup, with slight differences by brand (I've seen everything from 120 to 150 grams). **For this book, 1 cup all-purpose flour = 125 grams.**

GALETTE SEASONALITY GUIDE

Explore this chart to discover the best time for baking each galette based on produce seasonality. Most are accessible year-round, but for galettes made with hyperseasonal fruit and vegetables, check out the substitution options.

GALETTE	WINTER	SPRING	SUMMER	FALL	PRODUCE SUBSTITUTION OPTIONS
Almost Cannoli	X	X	X	X	
Apricot and Pepita-Sesame Frangipane		X	X		Use canned apricots if you can't find fresh. For fresh fruit, swap in peach, plum, or nectarine in summer into early fall; apple or pear in cooler seasons.
Beet, Cherry, and Radicchio	X	X	X	X	
Blue and Black Berries	X	X	X	X	Berries hit their peak in summer but are available year-round. (I don't recommend substituting frozen in this one.)
Brown-Buttered Apples and Honey	X	X	X	X	Apples are best in fall but are available year-round.
Buttered, Salted Radish	X	X	X	X	
Caramelized Zucchini and Bacon	X	X	X	X	Zucchini is best in summer but is available year-round.
Cheesy Ham and Eggs	X	X	X	X	
Chopped Mushroom and Kimchi	X	X	X	X	

GALETTE	WINTER	SPRING	SUMMER	FALL	PRODUCE SUBSTITUTION OPTIONS
Cocoa and Toasted Pecan	X	X	X	X	
Cottage Cheesy Greens with Chili Crisp	X	X	X	X	
Creamy Pistachio and Citrus	X	X	X	X	Citrus is best in winter but is available year-round.
Crumble-Topped Kabocha Squash	X			X	Kabocha squash is best in fall but can be accessible year-round. If you can't find it, swap in acorn, butternut, or delicata squash, or even sweet potatoes.
Figgy Miso			X	X	If you can't find fresh figs, swap in peach, plum, pear, or apple.
Gingery Cranberry Sauce	X	X	X	X	Fresh cranberries are plentiful in fall, but you can usually find frozen year-round. In spring, try swapping in strawberries and rhubarb (fresh or frozen).
Handheld Chocolate-Hazelnut	X	X	X	X	
Jammy Grape	X	X	X	X	Grapes are best in late summer into fall but are available year-round.
Leek and Sour Cream "Quiche"	X	X	X	X	
Lemony Spinach and Rice	X	X	X	X	
Lofty Peaches and Granola			X		Outside of peach season, use thawed frozen slices.
Marinated Artichoke and Tomato	X	X	X	X	
Minty Blueberry-Chamomile	X	X	X	X	Wild blueberries are best in summer but are available frozen or fresh year-round. If you can't find wild, see the recipe for how to best use larger varieties.
Mixed Sweet Potato and Harissa	X	X	X	X	

GALETTE	WINTER	SPRING	SUMMER	FALL	PRODUCE SUBSTITUTION OPTIONS
Not Quite Galette des Rois	X	X	X	X	
Pear with Sumac and Ginger	X	X	X	X	Pears are best in fall but are available year-round. If you can't find them, swap in apples or peaches.
Pepperoni Pizza	X	X	X	X	
Potato, Chips, and Red Onion	X	X	X	X	
Preserved Lemon Curd	X	X	X	X	
Raspberry and Rose	X	X	X	X	Raspberries are best in summer but are available year-round. Swap in frozen if the fresh ones look pale or underripe.
Rhubarb (or Persimmon!) with Halva	X	X	X	X	Use rhubarb in spring and summer; persimmon in fall and winter. If you can't find either, swap in peach, plum, pear, or apple.
Right-Side-Up Pineapple	X	X	X	X	Pineapple is best in spring into summer but is available year-round. Use canned pineapple if you can't find fresh.
Roasted and Raw Berry with Whole Lemon	X	X	X	X	Berries are best in summer but are available year-round. (I don't recommend substituting frozen in this one.)
Roasted and Raw Fennel	X	X	X	X	
Rotisserie Chicken, Potato, and Chèvre	X	X	X	X	
Scallion and Asparagus with Miso	X	X	X	X	In spring, swap in spring onions for the scallions.
Sharp Cheddar and Apple	X	X	X	X	Apples are best in fall but are available year-round.
Shredded Carrot with All the Herbs	X	X	X	X	
Smoky Cabbage and Chorizo	X	X	X	X	

GALETTE	WINTER	SPRING	SUMMER	FALL	PRODUCE SUBSTITUTION OPTIONS
Sour Cherry and Campari	X	X	X	X	Fresh sour cherries are available in spring and summer. Frozen sour cherries are accessible year-round but can be hard to find. To substitute, use a frozen tart-sweet cherry blend, canned tart cherries, or a mix of sweet cherries and cranberries.
Spice-Dusted Heirloom Tomato			X	X	Use Campari tomatoes if heirlooms aren't in season.
Spiced Cauliflower, Chickpeas, and Dates	X	X	X	X	
Spicy Eggplant Parm	X	X	X	X	Eggplant is best in summer but is available year-round.
Sticky Onion with Anchovies and Black Olives	X	X	X	X	
Sugared and Peppered Plum			X	X	If you remember, freeze your own plums (it's unlikely to find them packaged—see page 99 for the best method) and bake with them year-round. For fresh fruit, some supermarkets import plums in winter and fall; or swap in apples or pears.
Summer Squash and Any-Herb Pesto	X	X	X	X	Summer squash is best in summer but is available year-round.
Sweet Cherry and Lime	X	X	X	X	The recipe calls for frozen cherries—available year-round. In summer, try using fresh.
Vinegared Peppers and Big Beans	X	X	X	X	Peppers are best in summer but are available year-round.
Warm-Weather Tian	X	X	X	X	Eggplant, tomatoes, and zucchini are best in summer but are available year-round.
White Pie with Salad (and Maybe Mortadella)	X	X	X	X	In summer, add peach and/or plum wedges on top for bites of sweet with the salty.

A GOOD CRUST MAKES ALL THE DIFFERENCE

Making galette dough at home is as simple as mixing a few staple kitchen ingredients together with your hands. Pastry has a reputation for being finicky, but with a good recipe and a bit of practice, you'll never rely on store-bought dough again. (Save that for puff pastry or phyllo.)

Whether you're mixing together dry ingredients, cutting in butter, or folding together the final product, your fingers—as opposed to whisks, pastry blenders, or whirring blades—make it easier to tactilely understand what's happening. Get to know how the dough feels, and your galettes will turn out great. All that said, the process goes faster and requires less dexterity with a food processor (see page 31 for the method).

Galette pastry is essentially pie dough, of which there are several styles. From a traditional French baking perspective, pâte brisée, a pastry made of pea-sized pieces of cold fat cut into flour and salt and held together with water to create flaky layers, is the most common.

A Good Crust (opposite) is an even flakier variation on brisée: You'll want to leave the pieces of butter slightly larger than peas, around the size of a cannellini bean (I love legume-related references).

A GOOD CRUST

A galette is essentially half crust and half filling, so the dough's flavor is of the utmost importance. Butter, as opposed to shortening or another fat, makes the richest, most flavorful pastry. Sugar balances the salt and fat and aids a bit with browning—include it for sweet and savory galettes alike. Add a water-vinegar mixture by the splash for hydration (see page 28). Folding the dough over itself a few times (similar to a technique known as turning, more commonly found in pastry recipes like croissants or puff pastry) brings the mixture together and makes an extra-flaky crust.

The butter must stay cold in order for the dough to maintain its structure, then slowly melt and puff in the oven. To ensure this, chill the wet ingredients before they're incorporated and bring the dough together quickly. It's not a race, but don't stop for a phone call halfway through. Save that pause for after you've wrapped up the dough, when it absolutely needs at least 2 hours' rest to relax and hydrate completely before being rolled out.

This recipe makes enough dough for 2 standard galettes (or 4 tiny ones per disk of dough). Make one galette today, freeze a disk of dough for later. Alternatively, combine the entire batch of dough into one "XL" crust, for a sheet pan–sized slab or an extra-tall galette baked in a springform pan.

You can use this dough to make any galette in this book, but if you're interested in going the extra mile with a flavored crust, see the Variations (page 39).

Recipe continues

MAKES 2 STANDARD DISKS OR 1 XL DISK

½ cup (115 g) water

1 tablespoon apple cider vinegar

2¾ cups (345 g) spooned and leveled all-purpose flour, plus more as needed

1 tablespoon sugar

1½ teaspoons Diamond Crystal or ¾ teaspoon Morton kosher salt

2½ sticks (10 ounces/285 g) unsalted butter, cut into ½-inch (13 mm) cubes, chilled

1 In a liquid measuring cup or a small bowl, combine the water and the vinegar. Place this in the freezer while you work on the next steps.

2 In a large bowl, use your fingers or a fork to combine the flour, sugar, and salt.

3 Add the butter to the large bowl and use your fingers or a fork to gently toss around the butter to coat it in the flour mixture. Use your fingers to smash and rub the butter into the flour mixture until it forms flat pieces mostly the size of cannellini beans (about ¾ inch/2 cm) with some smaller (think chickpeas and lentils; about ½ and ¼ inch/13 and 6 mm). The mixture should still look dry and crumbly.

4 Remove the water-vinegar mixture from the freezer. Drizzle half of the water-vinegar mixture over the flour-butter mixture. Working from the bottom of the bowl up, use your fingers or a fork to gently toss the mixture together, as if you were tossing a salad. Drizzle over another splash of the water-vinegar mixture and toss. Continue to drizzle and toss until a shaggy, chunky mixture forms. It should not be completely combined yet, but there also should be no totally dry areas of flour (look for pebbles of moistened flour, not pure powder).

You may not need the full amount of water-vinegar mixture. When in doubt, err on the dry side: You can always add liquid, but you can't take it away.

5 Here's how to know if you're in a good place: Pick up a handful of the mixture and squish it. It should mostly hold its stuck-together shape; if not, drizzle an additional 1 teaspoon water-vinegar mixture on the driest areas and toss again, repeating until it holds together.

6 Dump the mixture onto a clean work surface and use your hands to pat it together into a rectangular mass about 1 inch (2.5 cm) thick. If you find any more areas that look totally dry, drizzle them with another 1 teaspoon water-vinegar mixture.

Recipe continues

Photos continue

7 Use your hands or a bench scraper to fold the mass of dough over itself. Press down the dough until it's about 1 inch (2.5 cm) thick again. (The dough shouldn't be moist or sticky, but if so, sprinkle it with a bit of flour as you fold.) Repeat folding and pressing down the dough two or three times. As you fold the dough over itself, the shaggy mass will form into a cohesive dough (this is also going to help the crust bake off extra-flaky). The butter should not blend all the way in, and the surface of the dough should look like marble or wood grain.

8 **If making a standard disk** (check your galette recipe): Divide the dough in half, placing each half on a piece of plastic wrap. **If making an XL disk** (check your galette recipe): Place the entire slab of dough on a piece of plastic wrap.

9 Wrap the dough in the plastic wrap, then press it into a round or rectangle (see Note) about ¾ inch (2 cm) thick. Refrigerate for at least 2 hours and up to 5 days. (Alternatively, freeze for up to 3 months; when you're ready to bake, see How to Thaw Frozen Galette Dough, page 33.)

NOTE: *Shaping your dough into the approximate shape of your galette (round, rectangular, etc.) will be helpful when rolling it out, but it's not imperative to achieve success. In fact, I typically shape my dough into squares for easy stacking in the freezer.*

How to Make a Good Crust in a Food Processor

There's no doubt that making galette dough goes faster with the help of a machine. Sometimes the process goes so fast that if you get distracted you can overwork the dough, but dare I say this technique is foolproof. I switch to this method when I'm making more than one batch of dough at a time, or if it's especially warm in the kitchen. If you're one of those people with "hot hands" who can't seem to smush butter without melting it, try this method. To ensure flaky layers, after processing the ingredients, bring the dough together as directed in step 7 on page 31 with a few folds. But if you really don't want to get your hands involved, transfer the crumbly dough directly from the food processor to plastic wrap and wrap it up. Gently roll over the wrapped dough with a rolling pin to ensure it's tightly pressed together and is about ¾ inch (2 cm) thick.

1 Freeze the cubed butter in a small bowl for 10 minutes. Prepare the water-vinegar mixture as written in the main recipe. Place the flour, sugar, and salt in the bowl of a food processor (at least 7-cup) and pulse three times to mix.

2 Add the chilled cubed butter (it should be firm but not frozen solid) to the food processor and pulse three or four times, for 1 second each, to first coat the butter in flour and then break it up into pieces roughly the size of chickpeas (about ½ inch/13 mm).

3 Remove the lid of the food processor and drizzle half of the water-vinegar mixture over the flour-butter mixture. Return the lid to the food processor and pulse two times, for 1 second each. Remove the lid and drizzle over another splash of the water-vinegar mixture. Pulse another two or three times, for 1 second each, to barely bring the mixture together (it should be crumbly, with moist pebbles of dough but no completely dry areas of flour). You may not use all of the water-vinegar mixture. If you see dry flour, mix in more of the water-vinegar mixture by the tablespoon with 1-second pulses.

4 Turn the dough out onto a clean work surface and break up any large pieces with your fingers or a bench scraper to make uniform crumbs. Continue on with the recipe from step 7. (The finished dough's butter pieces will be slightly smaller than if you made it by hand, and the dough's surface should look like terrazzo.)

WHAT'S THE DIFFERENCE BETWEEN AMERICAN- AND EUROPEAN-STYLE BUTTERS?

American-style butters are around 80 percent butterfat. The water content is higher than in European-style butters, and therefore American-style butters are firmer when cold and stay cold for longer out of the refrigerator. European-style butters have a higher (at least 82 percent) fat content, which makes a deeply flavorful, extra-crisp crust. Extra fat forms dough with a softer texture, making it slightly more challenging to work with (mitigate this by freezing the cubed butter for 10 minutes before incorporating it into the dough). See Resources (page 228) for my preferred brands.

WHAT'S THE DEAL WITH WATER?

Using too much water can lead to a tough pastry; too little and the crust will crack and crumble. What's more, every flour will hydrate differently, and different butters may change how the fat and flour incorporate. Further, if measuring flour in a measuring cup, there's a chance you'll scoop out more or less than you technically need. Because of these factors, it's best to start with less water and add more as needed. Getting comfortable with this process takes practice, but even if your crust ends up a little overhydrated (sticky to the touch or stretchy when rolling out) or underhydrated (so dry it cracks as it's rolled), it will still bake up all right. (A splash of vinegar added with the water slows the dough's oxidizing as it sits and adds nominal tenderizing properties and tangy flavor. If you don't have any, skip it.)

HOW TO THAW FROZEN GALETTE DOUGH

Remove the dough from the freezer and let it thaw in the refrigerator overnight. If you have less time, place the frozen dough on your kitchen counter and thaw until it's bendy, 2 to 4 hours. When going the room-temperature route, refrigerate the thawed dough for at least 20 minutes and up to 2 days before rolling it out to ensure it didn't get too warm.

ROLLING OUT THE DOUGH

Depending on which galette you're making, the dough will be rolled out a bit differently. Your galette recipe will note which of the following methods to use (**bookmark this page now**; **you'll be coming back to it**). If at any point your dough starts to get sticky during the rolling process (more likely to happen if your kitchen is warm or if you've used butter with a high fat content), return it to the plastic wrap or a sheet pan and refrigerate for at least 10 minutes to firm it back up, then pick up where you left off.

NOTE: *Galette dough bakes most successfully when it isn't overworked, and that applies to rolling as well. Apply firm, even pressure, and roll from the center of the dough out to the edges.*

BASIC METHOD: *For a round or rectangular free-form galette baked on a parchment-lined sheet pan. Use 1 standard disk (see photos, opposite).*

Remove the rested dough from the refrigerator and let it sit out for 5 to 10 minutes (this allows the dough to soften slightly, making it easier to roll out, without getting too warm). Line a sheet pan with parchment paper. Dust a work surface lightly with flour.

Unwrap the dough, sprinkle it with flour, and use a rolling pin to roll it out, flipping and turning the dough and adding more flour as needed to avoid sticking, into a round about 13½ inches (34 cm) in diameter and between ⅛ and ¼ inch (3 and 6 mm) thick; or a rectangle about 14 by 11 inches (33 by 28 cm) and between ⅛ and ¼ inch (3 and 6 mm) thick. If at any point the dough starts to crack, press it together with your fingers.

Gently fold the dough into quarters (this is just to help you move it; don't press down), place on the parchment-lined sheet pan, and unfold. From here, return to the galette recipe.

SLAB METHOD: *For an extra-large rectangular free-form galette (like slab pie!) baked on a parchment-lined sheet pan. Use 1 XL disk.*

Remove the rested dough from the refrigerator and let it sit out for 5 to 10 minutes (this allows the dough to soften slightly, making it easier to roll out, without getting too warm). Line a sheet pan with parchment paper. Dust a work surface lightly with flour.

Unwrap the dough, sprinkle it with flour, and use a rolling pin to roll it out, flipping and turning the dough and adding more flour as needed to avoid sticking, into a rectangle about 20 by 14 inches (50 by 36 cm) and between ⅛ and ¼ inch (3 and 6 mm) thick. If at any point the dough starts to crack, press it together with your fingers.

Gently fold the dough into quarters (this is just to help you move it; don't press down), place on the parchment-lined sheet pan, and unfold. From here, return to the galette recipe.

TINY METHOD: *For 1- or 2-serving free-form galettes baked on a parchment-lined sheet pan. One standard disk of dough makes 4 tiny galettes; one XL disk makes 8.*

Remove the rested dough from the refrigerator and let it sit out for 5 minutes (this allows the dough to soften slightly, making it easier to roll out, without getting too warm). Line a sheet pan with parchment paper. Dust a work surface lightly with flour.

Unwrap and cut a standard disk into 4 equal portions or cut an XL disk into 8 equal portions (about 95 g each). Use your hands and the work surface to shape the pieces into round disks. Sprinkle one piece of dough with flour and use a rolling pin to roll it out, flipping and turning the dough and adding more flour as needed to avoid sticking, into a round about 7 inches (18 cm) in diameter and ⅛ inch (3 mm) thick. If at any point the dough starts to crack, press it together with your fingers.

Repeat with the remaining dough pieces. If the kitchen is warm, transfer each rolled-out round to a large plate or sheet pan (it's okay to stack them) and set in the refrigerator while you finish rolling out the rest. From here, return to the galette recipe.

PAN METHOD: *For galettes baked in a greased 9- or 10-inch (23 or 25 cm) springform pan, cast-iron skillet, pie plate, tart pan, or cake pan.*

While you prepare the crust and filling, place an unlined sheet pan in the oven to preheat. (Placing the galette pan on a hot flat sheet pan will conduct more direct heat to the bottom of the vessel than oven grates alone will.) Don't skip this: The sheet pan will also catch any leaks that spring as the galette bakes, especially important for springform and tart pans, which have removable (not sealed) bottoms.

Remove the rested dough from the refrigerator and let it sit out for 5 to 10 minutes (this allows the dough to soften slightly, making it easier to roll out, without getting too warm). Dust a work surface lightly with flour.

Unwrap the dough, sprinkle it with flour, and use a rolling pin to roll it out, flipping and turning the dough and adding more flour as needed to avoid sticking, into a round about 13½ inches (34 cm) in diameter for a standard disk or 18 inches (46 cm) in diameter for an XL disk. Either version should be between ⅛ and ¼ inch (3 and 6 mm) thick. If at any point the dough starts to crack, press it together with your fingers.

Gently fold the dough into quarters (this is just to help you move it; don't press down), then drape it into the greased pan, letting it slump into the corners and hang over the rim. From here, return to the galette recipe.

WHY IS BUTTER LEAKING OUT OF MY GALETTE?

Sometimes you peek at your baking galette and notice it sitting in a pool of melted butter. "*Why?!*" you ask, shaking your fist at the sky. I hate to say it: This is one of those questions that doesn't have one definitive answer. Not working the butter well enough into the flour, not resting the dough for long enough, not chilling the dough or the filled galette properly, and not getting your oven hot enough are the main culprits when it comes to pooling butter. Has this happened to me? Of course. (And do I cry sometimes when it happens? Of course.) At the end of the day, not everything can be controlled, but it will not be the end of the world. The crust may turn out slightly tougher than desired, but your galette will still be perfectly tasty.

HOW TO BAKE GALETTES IN A MUFFIN TIN

For extra-small galettes that make a fun alternative to cupcakes or hors d'oeuvres for big gatherings, bake any fruit- or vegetable-based galette in a standard 12-cup muffin tin.

Remove the rested dough from the refrigerator and let it sit out for 5 minutes. Spray a 12-cup muffin tin with cooking spray or brush with neutral oil (if using a standard disk of dough, you'll only need to use 8 of the muffin tin's cups; if using an XL disk of dough, bake in two batches of 8). Dust a work surface lightly with flour.

Unwrap and cut a standard disk into 8 equal portions or cut an XL disk into 16 equal portions (about 50 g each). Use your hands and the work surface to shape the pieces into round disks. Sprinkle one piece of dough with flour and use a rolling pin to roll it out, flipping and turning the dough and adding more flour as needed to avoid sticking, into a round about 5½ inches (14 cm) in diameter and ⅛ inch (3 mm) thick. If at any point the dough starts to crack, press it together with your fingers.

Repeat with the remaining dough pieces. If the kitchen is warm, transfer each rolled-out round to a large plate or sheet pan (it's okay to stack them) and set in the refrigerator while you finish rolling out the rest.

Drape each dough round into the greased tin (work in batches as needed, storing extra dough rounds in the refrigerator), letting it slump into the corners of the cup and hang over the edges.

Fill each round with a scant ¼ cup (about 55 g; will differ slightly by individual filling) of prepared filling. Fold the edges of each round over the filling toward the center, overlapping and pleating as desired. Freeze the galettes for 10 minutes. Brush the edges of the dough with egg wash and sprinkle with sugar as you would with other sweet galettes.

Bake the galettes at 375°F (190°C) until the crust is deeply golden brown, 25 to 35 minutes, rotating the muffin tin front to back halfway through baking. Let the galettes cool for at least 15 minutes before twisting them out of the tins. Serve warm or cool completely. Store according to the directions in the main galette recipe.

FLAVORED CRUST VARIATIONS

Every galette in this book can be made with A Good Crust (page 27), but if you're itching to express additional creativity, you can inject a smidge of extra flavor and texture into the dough through seasonings and different flours. The flours all absorb liquid differently, so keep an eye on the adjusted water content—though you still may not use it all. If they're not called out below, all other ingredient amounts stay the same.

Cocoa Crust

A flash of cocoa powder adds a subtly bitter but not quite chocolaty richness to crust that complements extra-sweet fruit or nutty frangipane fillings. Dutch-process cocoa will make a darker brown crust than natural cocoa; whichever you use, make sure it's unsweetened.

Use 2½ cups plus 1 tablespoon (320 g) all-purpose flour and ⅓ cup (30 g) sifted natural or Dutch-process cocoa powder. Start with 9 tablespoons (130 g) water.

Whole Wheat Crust

Whole wheat flour contains the whole wheat kernel, making it higher in protein than all-purpose flour—great for dense, chewy bread. However, swapping in a bit of whole wheat flour makes for a crust that's still flaky but offers a nutty flavor that complements sweet and savory fillings.

Use 2 cups (250 g) all-purpose flour and ¾ cup (95 g) whole wheat flour. Start with 10 tablespoons (145 g) water.

Buckwheat Crust

Known as a pseudocereal, as it is not a grain but can be used as such, buckwheat has an earthy, almost bitter flavor. A buckwheat crust tempers the sweetness of frangipane, floral stone fruit, and root vegetables, making a second slice imperative.

Use 2 cups plus 1 tablespoon (260 g) all-purpose flour and ⅔ cup (85 g) buckwheat flour. Start with 10 tablespoons (145 g) water.

Cornmeal Crust

Cornmeal contributes a mild sweetness and a nubby texture to dough, plus a gentle golden tint. Try it with fillings that include citrus, stone fruit, berries, bitter greens, and tomatoes.

Use 2½ cups (315 g) all-purpose flour and ¼ cup (45 g) fine or medium-grind yellow cornmeal. Start with 9 tablespoons (130 g) water.

Warm-Spice Crust

A simple variation for sweet galettes, this fragrant pastry is delightful with autumnal cranberry, apple, and pear fillings.

Add ½ teaspoon each of ground cinnamon, cardamom, cloves, and allspice along with the flour.

Peppery Crust

Use this gently spiced crust variation with any savory galette, but don't sleep on trying it with sweet apple or stone fruit fillings.

Add 2 teaspoons coarsely ground black pepper along with the flour.

DRESSING UP GALETTES

A great galette doesn't need any accompaniment, but a crunchy topping sprinkled on prebake or a little dollop or drizzle of something before serving can result in a superior bite. Just about any fruit galette is improved with store-bought vanilla ice cream or a bowl of quickly whisked-together whipped cream; many a vegetable galette sings with no more than a squeeze of citrus or spoonful of yogurt. For a little extra effort and a lot of additional flavor, consider the following options.

CRUMBLE TOPPING

The beauty of a galette is that it doesn't need a top crust. However, to channel some vintage charm, try a crumble topping, which is baked onto the galette filling. (This mixture is also excellent sprinkled over single-layer cake or quick bread batter just before baking.)

Before assembling the galette filling, in a medium bowl, use a fork to mix together ¼ cup (30 g) all-purpose flour, ¼ cup (30 g) rolled oats, 3 tablespoons (40 g) light brown sugar, and ½ teaspoon Diamond Crystal or ¼ teaspoon Morton kosher salt. If you'd like a bit of warm fragrance, add ½ teaspoon each ground cinnamon and cardamom. Gently mix in 2½ tablespoons melted unrefined coconut oil or unsalted butter until the mixture forms large crumbs. Set aside while you prepare the rest of the galette.

Before pleating the crust, use your hands to scoop up big chunks of the crumble mixture and sprinkle it over the filling in bite-size pieces. Fold the edges of the crust over the crumble and filling toward the center, overlapping and pleating as desired, then continue with the galette recipe.

SAUCES AND DRIZZLES

If you want to go the extra mile, try making one of these sweet or savory condiments. Individual galette recipes will note which goes best with which.

TANGY SWEET CREAM: In a large bowl, whisk together 1 cup (230 g) heavy cream, 2 tablespoons powdered sugar, and a pinch of kosher salt until it forms soft peaks. Fold in ½ cup (115 g) sour cream, whole-milk ricotta, or whole-milk Greek yogurt until combined. The cream should be thick but dollop-able—if it's too stiff, fold in a bit more heavy cream by the tablespoon; too loose and you can whisk it for 10 to 30 seconds longer. Add more sugar to taste, then dollop over slices of galette. Store leftovers in an airtight container in the refrigerator for up to 24 hours. Makes about 2½ cups (340 g).

MAPLE WHIP: In a large bowl, whisk together 1½ cups (345 g) heavy cream, 2 tablespoons maple syrup or honey, 2 teaspoons vanilla extract, and a pinch of kosher salt until it forms soft peaks. Spoon over slices of galette. Store leftovers in an airtight container in the refrigerator for up to 24 hours. Makes about 3 cups (380 g).

NUTTY DRIZZLE: In a medium bowl, whisk together ¼ cup (65 g) tahini or your favorite unsweetened smooth nut or seed butter, 2 tablespoons water, 1 tablespoon honey or maple syrup, ¼ teaspoon each ground cinnamon and cardamom, ¼ teaspoon almond extract (optional), and a pinch of kosher salt until smooth, adding more water as needed until it reaches the consistency of caramel sauce. Spoon over slices of galette. Store leftovers in an airtight container in the refrigerator for up to 1 week. Makes about ⅓ cup (120 g).

AMARO BUTTERSCOTCH: In a medium saucepan, combine ½ cup (110 g) light brown sugar and 4 tablespoons (60 g) unsalted butter, cut into small pieces. Cook over medium heat, whisking occasionally, until the butter and sugar have melted, about 3 minutes. Slowly whisk in ½ cup (115 g) heavy cream, 2 tablespoons of your favorite amaro (or 1 tablespoon vanilla extract), and 1 teaspoon Diamond Crystal or ½ teaspoon Morton kosher salt. Bring to a boil, whisking constantly, and continue to cook until the butterscotch thickens enough to coat the back of a spoon, 6 to 8 minutes. Pour into a heatproof container and let cool for at least 15 minutes and up to 30 minutes (it will stiffen as it cools further). Drizzle warm over slices of galette. Store leftovers in an airtight container in the refrigerator for up to 2 weeks, rewarming over low heat on the stove if desired. Makes about ¾ cup (205 g).

ZINGY TAHINI: In a medium bowl, whisk together ¼ cup (65 g) tahini, 2 tablespoons fresh lime juice or rice vinegar, 1 teaspoon honey, and a big pinch of kosher salt until smooth. Add water as needed until it reaches the consistency of whole-milk yogurt. Season with more salt to taste.

Drizzle over slices of galette. Store leftovers in an airtight container in the refrigerator for up to 1 week. Makes about ½ cup (100 g).

GARLICKY YOGURT: In a medium bowl, whisk together 1 cup (230 g) whole-milk Greek yogurt or labneh, 2 tablespoons fresh lemon juice, 1 grated garlic clove, ¼ teaspoon Diamond Crystal or a pinch of Morton kosher salt, and a few grinds of freshly ground black pepper until smooth. Season with more salt and lemon juice to taste. Dollop over slices of galette. Store leftovers in an airtight container in the refrigerator for up to 2 days. Makes about 1 heaping cup (275 g).

CRISPY, FLAKY "SHORTBREAD"

A quick treat for when you don't feel like making a galette, or to make the most of any trimmings from A Good Crust (which can be baked immediately or frozen—no need to defrost).

Roll out 1 standard disk of A Good Crust (page 27) into a square between ⅛ and ¼ inch (3 and 6 mm) thick. Slice the dough into roughly 2-inch (5 cm) squares. Alternatively, use trimmings from crusts you've made, cut into similarly sized pieces. Arrange on a parchment-lined sheet pan, spaced at least ¼ inch (6 mm) apart, and freeze for 10 minutes while you preheat the oven to 375°F (190°C).

Brush the top of each square with egg wash (a great use for leftovers from your last galette). Sprinkle with granulated or demerara sugar and flaky sea salt for a sweet treat or with coarsely ground black pepper (or any crushed fragrant seed, like fennel, cumin, or coriander) and flaky sea salt to keep things savory. Bake until golden brown, 12 to 20 minutes (lower end for small pieces, higher end if baking from frozen). Remove from the oven and let the shortbread cool for 10 minutes, then serve. These are best eaten day-of; store leftovers in an airtight container at room temperature for up to 2 days.

STONE
FRUIT

Sugared and Peppered Plum
50

Lofty Peaches and Granola
53

Sweet Cherry and Lime
55

Apricot and Pepita-Sesame
Frangipane
58

Sour Cherry and Campari
61

Stone fruit is an umbrella term for peaches, plums, nectarines, cherries, and apricots, or fruit with a fleshy exterior and a single pit, aka stone. These special fruits are juicy and sweet, making an ideal filling for galettes. To best harness stone fruits' flavor, bake with them during the height of their abundance. Bonus: This is also when they're most affordable (admittedly a relative term).

When shopping for fresh stone fruit, look for unblemished skin with some give when pressed—not rock-hard and not mushy. When it comes to peaches, plums, and nectarines, if you're not baking immediately, you can buy firm, underripe fruit and place them in a paper bag at room temperature until they become fragrant and soft. In a pinch, you can use slightly underripe stone fruit in galettes—the less-developed raw flavor will deepen as the fruit bakes with sugar. Extremely overripe fruit, however, can go too soft in the oven and make for a soggy galette if used raw. Instead, first turn it into a quick jam by boiling a ratio of two parts chopped fruit and one part granulated sugar with a bit of lemon juice and salt until soft and thick. Cool, then spoon ½ cup (about 170 g) of the jam into the base of a galette topped with another sliced fruit and bake according to The Anything Goes Galette (page 132).

SUGARED AND PEPPERED PLUM

SERVES 6 TO 8

2 pounds (910 g) fresh plums
   (8 to 14), pitted and halved
   (quartered if larger than
   2 inches/5 cm)

⅓ cup (65 g) sugar, plus more
   for sprinkling

2 tablespoons chopped fresh
   tarragon (optional)

1 tablespoon dry vermouth or
   apple cider vinegar

1 tablespoon cornstarch

¾ teaspoon coarsely ground
   black pepper

½ teaspoon Diamond Crystal or
   ¼ teaspoon Morton kosher
   salt

1 standard disk A Good Crust
   (page 27)

Egg wash: 1 large egg, beaten

Fennel seeds (optional)

Good extra-virgin olive oil
   (optional), for serving

**CRUST VARIATION
OPTION:** Buckwheat
(page 39)

Plums just *belong* in galettes. The tart, floral orbs practically beg to be swaddled in buttery pastry. The beet-red flesh of Black Splendor plums (which you can find at the supermarket in season) is especially gorgeous when it comes to contrasting color with the crust. But why not play around with a handful of varieties if you can find them? Whichever plums you choose, dress them with black pepper and a splash of herbal dry vermouth.

Call it gilding the lily, but instead of ice cream or whipped cream, a slice is excellent topped with freshly shaved Parmesan and a drizzle of honey in addition to the grassy olive oil.

1 Preheat the oven to 425°F (220°C) with a rack positioned in the center. Line a sheet pan with parchment paper.

2 In a large bowl, toss together the plums, sugar, tarragon (if using), vermouth, cornstarch, pepper, and salt.

3 Roll the dough into a round and set it on the lined sheet pan using the Basic Method (page 34).

4 Spoon the filling into the crust, leaving a 2-inch (5 cm) border. Fold the edges of the crust over the filling toward the center, overlapping and pleating as desired. Freeze the galette on the sheet pan for 10 minutes.

5 Remove the galette from the freezer and brush the egg wash over the exposed crust. Sprinkle fennel seeds (if using) and more sugar over the crust.

6 Bake until the crust is starting to turn golden, 12 to 15 minutes. Reduce the oven temperature to 375°F (190°C) and continue to bake until the plums have softened and the crust is deeply golden brown, another 40 to 50 minutes, rotating the pan front to back halfway through.

7 Remove the galette from the oven and cool, uncovered, for at least 25 minutes and up to 8 hours.

8 Slice and serve, with a drizzle of olive oil if desired.

Leftovers can be stored at room temperature, loosely covered, for up to 2 days. Reheat on a sheet pan in a 350°F (180°C) oven until warmed through, about 10 minutes.

VARIATION

For a bit more sweetness and texture, add the Crumble Topping (page 41).

WHY FREEZE A GALETTE BEFORE BAKING?

You'll notice that every galette is popped in the freezer before it's baked. Rolling out the crust, filling it, and folding up the edges is quite a lot of handling for a delicate buttery pastry. The warmer the dough gets, the higher the risk of butter melting into the flour, preventing lovely flaky layers of crust from forming as it bakes. Galettes also expand in the oven, so when filled especially full without setting up in the freezer, they can potentially unfold as they bake, spilling your hard work all over the sheet pan. Can you skip the big chill? The risk is yours. If you don't have space in your freezer for a sheet pan, try freezing the galette (on the parchment) on a flat plate or cutting board, or refrigerate the galette on the sheet pan for double the indicated freezing time.

LOFTY PEACHES AND GRANOLA

Baked in a springform pan for slices that rival the height of layer cake, this peach number is a showstopper. The delicately sweet fruit (white versions of which slant floral, whereas yellow peaches offer more tang) is a natural partner to a buttery, ideally whole wheat flour–laced, crust. Below the peach wedges you'll find a layer of granola, which hangs on to some of its crunch even when covered by roasting fruit. Opt for a granola brand with lots of nuts and seeds for the most exciting flavor and varying textures. Dollop slices with plain yogurt for an unbeatable late-summer breakfast.

NOTE: *If the craving strikes when peaches aren't in season, use frozen peach slices, which are preserved at their ripest and most flavorful. Frozen fruit tends to deflate more than fresh as it bakes, so use a bit more than the fresh version: Thaw 3 pounds (1.36 kg) frozen peach slices in their bag in the refrigerator overnight, then drain in a colander and dry on paper towels or kitchen towels. Bake, tented with foil as needed, for an extra 10 to 15 minutes to ensure a crisp bottom crust.*

SERVES 8 TO 10

- ⅓ cup (65 g) sugar, plus more for sprinkling
- 2 tablespoons grated lemon or lime zest
- 3 tablespoons (25 g) cornstarch
- 2½ pounds (1.1 kg) peaches and/or nectarines (about 6 medium), peeled if desired, pitted, and sliced into ¼-inch (6 mm) wedges
- 2 tablespoons fresh lemon or lime juice
- 1 teaspoon Diamond Crystal or ½ teaspoon Morton kosher salt
- ¼ teaspoon almond extract, or 1 teaspoon vanilla extract
- Cooking spray or vegetable oil, for the pan
- 1 XL disk A Good Crust (page 27), preferably the Whole Wheat variation
- 1 cup (120 g) of your favorite granola, any large clumps broken up, plus more for serving
- Egg wash: 1 large egg, beaten

1 Preheat the oven to 425°F (220°C) with a rack positioned in the center. Place a sheet pan in the oven to preheat.

2 In a large bowl, combine the sugar and zest and rub with your fingers until the sugar is slightly moistened and fragrant. Stir in the cornstarch, then toss in the peaches, citrus juice, salt, and extract.

Recipe continues

SPECIAL EQUIPMENT:
9- or 10-inch (23 or 25 cm)
springform pan

**CRUST VARIATION
OPTION:** Whole Wheat
(page 39), Cornmeal (page 39)

SERVE WITH: Vanilla ice
cream, plain yogurt, Tangy Sweet
Cream (page 42), or Nutty Drizzle
(page 42)

3 Grease a 9- or 10-inch (23 or 25 cm) springform pan with cooking spray. Roll the dough into a round and fit it into the pan using the Pan Method (page 36).

4 Sprinkle the granola over the base of the crust. Leaving any excess liquid in the bowl, spoon the peach filling over the granola. Use kitchen scissors to trim the edges of the dough so it can fold over the filling by about 2 inches (5 cm). (Save the trimmings for Crispy, Flaky "Shortbread," page 45.) Fold the edges of the crust over the filling toward the center, overlapping and pleating as desired. Freeze the galette for 10 minutes.

5 Remove the galette from the freezer and brush the egg wash over the exposed crust. Sprinkle more sugar over the crust.

6 Place the springform pan on the preheated sheet pan in the oven. Bake until the crust is starting to turn golden, 12 to 15 minutes. Reduce the oven temperature to 375°F (190°C) and continue to bake until the filling is bubbling and the crust is deeply golden brown and starting to pull away from the edges of the pan, another 65 to 75 minutes, rotating the pan front to back halfway through. If the exposed filling or crust starts to singe in places before 60 minutes, tent with foil and continue baking.

7 Remove the galette from the oven and cool, uncovered, for at least 2 hours and up to 8 hours before unmolding. Slice and serve, topped with more granola.

Leftovers can be stored at room temperature, loosely covered, for up to 2 days. Reheat on a sheet pan in a 350°F (180°C) oven until warmed through, about 10 minutes.

SWEET CHERRY AND LIME

Like their fellows in the stone fruit realm, dark, sweet cherries boast a remarkable depth of flavor that is somehow more vibrant when roasted. Here's a secret: I rarely bother using fresh cherries in a galette. Pitting pounds of the fruit takes a lot of time and dexterity, not to mention their magenta juice gets on everything. In peak season, fresh cherries can be quite pricey, and you might as well just eat them raw, still sun-warmed, on your way home from the market. That said, you *can* use fresh here (grab an extra few ounces to compensate for the pits and inevitable snacking).

1 Preheat the oven to 425°F (220°C) with a rack positioned in the center. Line a sheet pan with parchment paper.

2 In a large bowl, combine the sugar, lime zest, and ginger and rub with your fingers until the sugar is slightly moistened and fragrant. Stir in the cornstarch, lime juice, vanilla, almond extract (if using), and kosher salt until combined. Stir in the cherries and coat completely in the sugar mixture.

3 Roll the dough into a round and set it on the lined sheet pan using the Basic Method (page 34).

4 Leaving any excess liquid in the bowl, spoon the filling into the crust, leaving a 2-inch (5 cm) border (it may not look like enough cherries, but trust that they'll swell and deflate as they bake). Fold the edges of the crust over the filling toward the center, overlapping and pleating as desired. Freeze the galette on the sheet pan for 10 minutes.

Recipe continues

SERVES 6 TO 8

⅓ cup (65 g) sugar, plus more for sprinkling

1 tablespoon grated lime zest

1 tablespoon finely grated fresh ginger, or ¼ teaspoon ground ginger

¼ cup (30 g) cornstarch

2 tablespoons fresh lime juice

1 teaspoon vanilla extract

½ teaspoon almond extract (optional)

½ teaspoon Diamond Crystal or ¼ teaspoon Morton kosher salt, plus more to taste

1¼ pounds (565 g) pitted frozen or fresh sweet cherries (about 4 heaping cups)

1 standard disk A Good Crust (page 27)

Egg wash: 1 large egg, beaten

Flaky sea salt, for sprinkling

CRUST VARIATION OPTIONS: Buckwheat (page 39), Cocoa (page 39)

SERVE WITH: Vanilla ice cream or Tangy Sweet Cream (page 42), a damn fine cup of coffee

5 Remove the galette from the freezer and brush the egg wash over the exposed crust. Sprinkle more sugar over the crust.

6 Bake until the crust is starting to turn golden, 12 to 15 minutes (if using a cocoa crust variation, look for the crust to darken slightly). Reduce the oven temperature to 375°F (190°C) and continue to bake until the fruit is slightly bubbling and the crust is deeply golden brown, another 40 to 50 minutes, rotating the pan front to back halfway through.

7 Remove the galette from the oven and sprinkle with some flaky sea salt. Cool, uncovered, for at least 25 minutes and up to 8 hours.

8 Slice and serve.

Leftovers can be stored at room temperature, loosely covered, for up to 2 days. Reheat on a sheet pan in a 350°F (180°C) oven until warmed through, about 10 minutes.

VARIATION

Fresh raspberries, blackberries, and/or halved strawberries swap in for the cherries beautifully.

APRICOT AND PEPITA-SESAME FRANGIPANE

SERVES 6 TO 8

½ cup (100 g) sugar, plus more for sprinkling

½ cup (60 g) unsalted roasted pepitas or sunflower seeds

3 tablespoons (30 g) buckwheat flour

½ teaspoon Diamond Crystal or ¼ teaspoon Morton kosher salt

¼ cup (65 g) tahini

2 tablespoons unsalted butter, cut into small pieces, at room temperature

2 large eggs

¼ teaspoon rose water or almond extract (optional; see Note)

3 tablespoons (25 g) sesame seeds

1 standard disk A Good Crust (page 27)

3 to 4 apricots (about 7 ounces/ 200 g), pitted (no need to peel) and quartered (about 1 cup)

Flaky sea salt

CRUST VARIATION OPTION: Cornmeal (page 39)

Bookmark this to make when you want to show off. The crust is filled with a thick layer of toasted seed frangipane with a touch of earthy buckwheat flour and rose water—sounds complicated, but it's wildly simple. Petite apricot wedges stud the filling, making each bite floral and not too sweet. After tasting dozens of galettes, I never (ever) turn down a slice of this one.

If you can't find fresh apricots, which are challenging to score out of season, try canned. Look for apricot halves in juice or light syrup. Drain and dry them on a towel-lined plate, slice, and you're good to go.

NOTE: *Rose water, a fragrant liquid generated through steam distillation of rose petals, can be used like an extract in cooking. It's quite strong, so a little goes a long way: Think of it more like almond extract than vanilla. (That said, if you don't like rose or almond, skip them or use ½ teaspoon vanilla extract instead.)*

1 In a food processor, combine the sugar, pepitas, buckwheat flour, and kosher salt and pulse until the mixture is finely ground, like almond flour. Pulse in the tahini, butter, 1 of the eggs, and the rose water (if using) until mostly smooth. Pulse in 2 tablespoons of the sesame seeds until just combined but not blended. If not baking the galette immediately, refrigerate the frangipane in an airtight container for up to 1 week; bring to room temperature by letting it sit out until spreadable (for up to 2 hours) before using.

2 Preheat the oven to 425°F (220°C) with a rack positioned in the center. Line a sheet pan with parchment paper.

Recipe continues

3 Roll the dough into a round and set it on the lined sheet pan using the Basic Method (page 34).

4 Spoon the frangipane into the crust, leaving a 2-inch (5 cm) border. Arrange the apricots cut-side up over the filling evenly in a single layer (there will be some open spaces where the filling is visible). Fold the edges of the crust over the filling toward the center, overlapping and pleating as desired. Freeze the galette on the sheet pan for 10 minutes.

5 In a small bowl, beat the remaining egg to make an egg wash. Remove the galette from the freezer and brush the egg wash over the exposed crust. Sprinkle the remaining 1 tablespoon sesame seeds over the crust, then more sugar over the entire galette.

6 Bake until the crust is starting to turn golden, 12 to 15 minutes. Reduce the oven temperature to 375°F (190°C) and continue to bake until the crust is deeply golden brown and the filling has puffed, another 25 to 35 minutes, rotating the pan front to back halfway through.

7 Remove the galette from the oven and sprinkle with some flaky sea salt. Cool, uncovered, for at least 15 minutes and up to 8 hours.

8 Slice and serve.

Leftovers can be stored in an airtight container in the refrigerator or at room temperature for up to 3 days. Reheat on a sheet pan in a 350°F (180°C) oven until warmed through, about 10 minutes.

SOUR CHERRY AND CAMPARI

I typically prefer to save alcohol for glasses (especially poured over ice) but there are a few instances where spirits excel in desserts. This Campari-spiked galette is one. The herbal aperitif, tart cherries, and floral citrus zest all point to the fact that this is a pastry for those who prefer bitter to sweet. Scarlet-red sour cherries—completely different in flavor from their sweet magenta counterparts—tend to pop up at grocery stores and farmers markets for a month or so in summer. When you find them, buy as many pounds as your tote bag can fit, round up a few friends, and get to work pitting.

1 In a medium saucepan, combine the sugar, zest, and salt and rub with your fingers until the sugar is slightly moistened and fragrant. Stir in the cherries. Heat the mixture over medium-high heat and cook, stirring often with a spatula to ensure the mixture doesn't burn (try not to smush the cherries), until the cherries have softened and the released liquid is bubbling, 8 to 12 minutes.

2 In a small bowl, stir together the cornstarch and 2 tablespoons of the Campari until it forms a smooth slurry. Stir the slurry into the cherry mixture and reduce the heat to medium-low. Continue to cook, stirring often, until the mixture gets very thick and jammy, 4 to 6 minutes. You should be able to drag a spatula through the mixture and cleanly see the bottom of the pot as the filling slowly oozes over. Remove from the heat and stir in the remaining 1 tablespoon Campari.

3 Meanwhile, set up a large bowl of ice and water for an ice bath.

Recipe continues

SERVES 6 TO 8

⅓ cup (65 g) sugar, plus more for sprinkling

1 tablespoon grated blood orange or grapefruit zest

½ teaspoon Diamond Crystal or ¼ teaspoon Morton kosher salt

1¼ pounds (565 g) pitted fresh or frozen sour cherries (about 4 heaping cups)

2 tablespoons cornstarch

3 tablespoons (40 g) Campari or Aperol (or fresh blood orange or grapefruit juice)

1 standard disk A Good Crust (page 27)

Egg wash: 1 large egg, beaten

CRUST VARIATION OPTION: Cornmeal (page 39)

SERVE WITH: Vanilla ice cream or unsweetened whipped cream

4 Scrape the mixture into a medium bowl placed over the bowl of ice water and let cool to room temperature, about 20 minutes. If not making the galette right away, refrigerate the mixture in an airtight container for up to 1 week.

5 When you're ready to bake, preheat the oven to 425°F (220°C) with a rack positioned in the center. Line a sheet pan with parchment paper.

6 Roll the dough into a round and set it on the lined sheet pan using the Basic Method (page 34).

7 Spoon the filling into the crust, leaving a 2-inch (5 cm) border. Fold the edges of the crust over the filling toward the center, overlapping and pleating as desired. Freeze the galette on the sheet pan for 10 minutes.

8 Remove the galette from the freezer and brush the egg wash over the exposed crust. Sprinkle more sugar over the crust.

9 Bake until the crust is starting to turn golden, 12 to 15 minutes. Reduce the oven temperature to 375°F (190°C) and continue to bake until the crust is deeply golden brown and the filling is bubbling, another 35 to 45 minutes, rotating the pan front to back halfway through.

10 Remove the galette from the oven and cool, uncovered, for at least 25 minutes and up to 8 hours.

11 Slice and serve.

Leftovers can be stored at room temperature, loosely covered, for up to 2 days. Reheat on a sheet pan in a 350°F (180°C) oven until warmed through, about 10 minutes.

WHY USE AN ICE BATH?

A just-cooked galette filling must cool completely before it's added to the crust, hence placing it in a bowl of ice water. The technique saves time and ensures the filling cools quickly enough to prevent growing harmful bacteria.

ON THE FLEETING BEAUTY OF SEASONAL FRUIT

When I see hyperseasonal fruit, I get giddy. All year long,* at whichever market (super, farmers) I find myself strolling through, there's at least one citrus or berry that wasn't there last week—and there may not be any left tomorrow. I will always buy a few pounds without a plan and eventually make a galette just as the fruit turns ripe, snacking on about as much of it fresh as I tuck into pastry.

Thanks to increased importation, technological advances in refrigeration, and general impatience, myriad varieties of fruit pop up outside of the time and place they'd naturally grow. This is why those of us who live in New York can still find fresh plums in December. Still, as anyone who's eaten a December plum (or strawberry or fig, for that matter) can attest to, the flavor is barely comparable to those available in their local growing season. When you find such precious specimens, treat them exceptionally kindly—naturally an excellent suggestion is to wrap them in a cocoon of A Good Crust and bake until soft. Shingle May's Barbie-pink rhubarb—or November's silky Fuyu persimmons—over crumbled halva (page 122); in July, use perfectly plump berries in the baked filling *and* raw as a topping (page 96). And those late-August plums? Toss them with tarragon-seasoned sugar and black pepper (page 50).

Of course, if you happen to overbuy some especially lovely produce at the farmers market, fruit freezes well, and most varieties bake up delightfully in a galette. For hot tips on freezing fruit, head to When and How to Galette with Frozen Fruit (page 99).

*Making an exception for the doldrums of winter, when sometimes weeks can go by with only a bit of produce variation. For moments like that, check out the Apples, Pears, and Citrus chapter (page 66), which makes the most of fresh fruit that is just about as good in February as it is in September.

APPLES, PEARS, AND CITRUS

Creamy Pistachio and Citrus
70

Sharp Cheddar and Apple
73

Pear with Sumac and Ginger
75

Preserved Lemon Curd
78

Brown-Buttered Apples and Honey
81

L et's hear it for the fruit that stays bakeable for weeks: I'm talking apples, pears, and citrus. You know them, you like them, you buy them. Forget about them during a busy few weeks, rediscover them in your crisper, and miracle: They're still fresh and ready to become a galette. Unlike delicate berries and ripe stone fruit, these workhorses of the produce department can even survive being dropped from your grocery bag without the risk of smushing. Plus, they tend to be available at just about any store, any time of year. To ensure that long life, keep them in the cold, dark refrigerator.

Apples and pears can handle becoming the bulk of a galette filling—slice and bake them at a moment's notice. Varieties are plentiful depending on the season, but certain types, like Honeycrisp and Pink Lady apples or Bosc and Anjou pears, hold on to their crisp texture best during a galette's long journey in the oven without going dry or mealy (the horror). Apples and pears are also interchangeable in this chapter's recipes, so go ahead and play.

Citrus works wonders as a galette-filling component as opposed to a solo venture: Spoon frangipane or creamy curd into the crust first, then layer on bittersweet grapefruit, any variety of orange, even lemons, feeling free to mix and match.

CREAMY PISTACHIO AND CITRUS

SERVES 6 TO 8

1¼ cups (170 g) unsalted roasted pistachios or hazelnuts

⅓ cup (65 g) sugar, plus more for sprinkling

3 tablespoons (45 g) unsalted butter, at room temperature

3 tablespoons (35 g) semolina flour (or 2 tablespoons fine-grind cornmeal plus 1 tablespoon all-purpose flour)

2 large eggs

1 tablespoon Grand Marnier or Cointreau, or 2 teaspoons orange blossom water

1 teaspoon Diamond Crystal or ½ teaspoon Morton kosher salt

1 to 2 medium grapefruit and/or oranges (about 7 ounces/200 g), peeled if desired, thinly sliced into rounds, any seeds removed

Cooking spray or vegetable oil, for the pan

1 standard disk A Good Crust (page 27)

¼ cup (145 g) orange marmalade

Mild chile flakes, such as Aleppo pepper (optional), for serving

Wintry citrus-heavy fruit salads serve as inspiration here. On cold mornings, a plate of grapefruit and oranges (Cara Cara, blood, and mandarin varieties are particularly special) with buttery crushed nuts and a dusting of chile flakes warms my body and heart. You'll notice a similar sensation when these ingredients find their way into a galette.

Under the blanket of pink and orange fruit is a sage-green pistachio frangipane, enhanced with a flash of orange liqueur. Dotting sweet marmalade over the top before baking brings grapefruit brûlée vibes, without any overtly 1970s energy.

NOTE: *If you can only find salted roasted nuts, use them, and skip the additional salt in the frangipane; or toast your own nuts from raw (see Nuts and Seeds, page 19).*

1 In a food processor, combine the pistachios, sugar, butter, semolina flour, 1 of the eggs, the Grand Marnier, and salt and pulse until mostly smooth. If not baking the galette immediately, refrigerate the frangipane in an airtight container for up to 1 week, and bring to room temperature by letting it sit out until spreadable (for up to 2 hours) before using.

2 When you're ready to bake, place the citrus slices on a paper towel or kitchen towel to drain for at least 5 minutes.

3 Preheat the oven to 425°F (220°C) with a rack positioned in the center. Place a sheet pan in the oven to preheat.

4 Grease a 9- or 10-inch (23 or 25 cm) cast-iron skillet, pie plate, or cake pan with cooking spray. Roll the dough into a round and fit it into the pan using the Pan Method (page 36).

5 Spoon the frangipane into the crust, then arrange the sliced citrus over the frangipane in a single layer (feel free to slightly overlap, but you may not use it all). Dollop the marmalade over the citrus. Fold the edges of the crust over the filling toward the center, overlapping and pleating as desired. Freeze the galette for 10 minutes.

6 In a small bowl, beat the remaining egg to make an egg wash. Remove the galette from the freezer and brush the egg wash over the exposed crust. Sprinkle more sugar over the crust.

7 Place the skillet on the preheated sheet pan in the oven. Bake until the crust is starting to turn golden, 12 to 15 minutes (if using a cocoa crust variation, look for the crust to darken slightly). Reduce the oven temperature to 375°F (190°C) and continue to bake until the filling has puffed and the crust is deeply golden brown, another 30 to 40 minutes, rotating the pan front to back halfway through. (If the filling produces an air bubble at any point, carefully poke it with a paring knife to release.)

8 Remove the galette from the oven and cool, uncovered, for at least 30 minutes and up to 8 hours.

9 Slice and serve, sprinkled with chile flakes (if using).

Leftovers can be stored in an airtight container in the refrigerator for up to 2 days. Reheat on a sheet pan in a 350°F (180°C) oven until warmed through, about 10 minutes.

SPECIAL EQUIPMENT:
9- or 10-inch (23 or 25 cm) cast-iron skillet, metal or ceramic pie plate, or cake pan

CRUST VARIATION OPTIONS: Cocoa (page 39), Cornmeal (page 39)

SHARP CHEDDAR AND APPLE

Just as welcome at brunch as it is on the dessert table, this savory-slanting sweet galette riffs on the centuries-old tradition of topping a slice of apple pie with Cheddar. Splurge on the clothbound style of cheese if you can find it: Its complex-yet-approachable funk and nuttiness know how to dance with apple and maple syrup. Bake this one in a skillet, pie plate, or cake pan for a thicker wedge, or go free-form for classic galette vibes.

1 Preheat the oven to 425°F (220°C) with a rack positioned in the center. If baking in a vessel, place a sheet pan in the oven to preheat; otherwise, line a sheet pan with parchment paper and set it on a work surface.

2 In a large bowl, toss together the apples, Cheddar, maple syrup, cornstarch, thyme (if using), vinegar, and kosher salt.

3 If using, grease a 9- or 10-inch (23 or 25 cm) cast-iron skillet, pie plate, or cake pan with cooking spray. Roll the dough into a round and fit it into the vessel using the Pan Method (page 36). Alternatively, for a free-form galette, roll the dough into a round and set it on the lined sheet pan using the Basic Method (page 34).

4 Pour the filling into the crust (leaving a 2-inch/5 cm border if free-form). Fold the edges of the crust over the filling toward the center, overlapping and pleating as desired. Freeze the galette for 10 minutes.

5 Remove the galette from the freezer and brush the egg wash over the exposed crust. Sprinkle sugar, flaky salt, and pepper over the entire galette.

Recipe continues

SERVES 6 TO 8

1½ pounds (680 g) crisp, sweet apples (about 4 medium), such as Honeycrisp or Pink Lady, cored and cut into ¼ inch (6 mm) slices (no need to peel)

¾ cup (100 g) crumbled Cheddar cheese, preferably clothbound or extra-sharp, plus more for serving

3 tablespoons (60 g) maple syrup

2 tablespoons cornstarch

1 tablespoon finely chopped fresh thyme leaves (optional)

1 tablespoon apple cider vinegar

½ teaspoon Diamond Crystal or ¼ teaspoon Morton kosher salt, plus more to taste

Cooking spray or vegetable oil, as needed

1 standard disk A Good Crust (page 27)

Egg wash: 1 large egg, beaten

Demerara or granulated sugar

Flaky sea salt

Coarsely ground black pepper

SPECIAL EQUIPMENT (OPTIONAL): 9- or 10-inch (23 or 25 cm) cast-iron skillet, metal or ceramic pie plate, or cake pan

CRUST VARIATION OPTION: Peppery (page 40)

SERVE WITH: Amaro Butterscotch (page 42) or Nutty Drizzle (page 42)

6 If baking in a vessel, place it on the preheated sheet pan in the oven; if baking free-form, place the sheet pan in the oven. Bake until the crust is starting to turn golden, 12 to 15 minutes. Reduce the oven temperature to 375°F (190°C) and continue to bake until the crust is deeply golden and the filling takes on color (and starts to pull away from the sides of the skillet if using), another 50 to 60 minutes in the skillet or pie plate, or 40 to 50 minutes free-form, rotating the sheet pan front to back halfway through. (If you find the apples are starting to singe before the lowest time cue, tent the exposed filling with foil and continue baking.)

7 Remove the galette from the oven and cool, uncovered, for at least 30 minutes and up to 2 hours.

8 Slice and serve, topped with more crumbled Cheddar.

Leftovers can be stored in an airtight container in the refrigerator for up to 2 days. Reheat on a sheet pan in a 350°F (180°C) oven until warmed through, about 10 minutes.

VARIATION

For a bit more sweetness and texture, add the Crumble Topping (page 41).

PEAR WITH SUMAC AND GINGER

With its short ingredient list and simple technique, this galette is a lesson in chilling out. Toss tart sumac and ground ginger with salt and sugar for a sparkly pink mixture that tastes like a less-saccharine coating for sour gummy candy. Shower the seasoned sugar under and over thinly sliced pears (feel free to swap in apples or firm peaches) and you're ready to bake. Serve it warm and a scoop of vanilla ice cream will melt into a delightful puddle of sweet cream over the tiled fruit slices.

NOTE: *Sumac is a dried and ground berry that's deep crimson in color and lemony-tart in flavor. It's commonly used in savory Levantine dishes but also adds a lovely brightness to sweets.*

1 Preheat the oven to 425°F (220°C) with a rack positioned in the center. Line a sheet pan with parchment paper.

2 Slice the pears lengthwise off the core into 4 lobes. Slice each lobe lengthwise ⅛ inch (3 mm) thick, keeping the bundles together. In a small bowl, combine the sugar, sumac, ginger, and kosher salt.

3 Roll the dough into a round and set it on the lined sheet pan using the Basic Method (page 34).

4 Sprinkle 2 tablespoons of the sugar mixture over the crust, leaving a 2-inch (5 cm) border. Fan out the pear bundles in varying directions over the sugar. Sprinkle the remaining sugar mixture over the pears. Fold the edges of the crust over the filling toward the center, overlapping and pleating as desired. Freeze the galette on the sheet pan for 10 minutes.

Recipe continues

SERVES 6 TO 8

1¼ pounds (565 g) Bosc, Anjou, and/or Asian pears (about 3)

3 tablespoons (40 g) sugar

1 tablespoon ground sumac (see Note)

2 teaspoons ground ginger

½ teaspoon Diamond Crystal or ¼ teaspoon Morton kosher salt

1 standard disk A Good Crust (page 27)

Egg wash: 1 large egg, beaten

Flaky sea salt

CRUST VARIATION OPTIONS: Whole Wheat (page 39), Warm-Spice (page 40)

SERVE WITH: Vanilla ice cream, Amaro Butterscotch (page 42), or Maple Whip (page 42)

5 Remove the galette from the freezer and brush the egg wash over the exposed crust.

6 Bake until the crust is starting to turn golden, 12 to 15 minutes. Reduce the oven temperature to 375°F (190°C) and continue to bake until the pears are tender and the crust is deeply golden brown, another 35 to 45 minutes, rotating the pan front to back halfway through.

7 Remove the galette from the oven and sprinkle with some flaky sea salt. Cool, uncovered, for at least 20 minutes and up to 8 hours.

8 Slice and serve.

Leftovers can be stored at room temperature, loosely covered, for up to 2 days. Reheat on a sheet pan in a 350°F (180°C) oven until warmed through, about 10 minutes.

VARIATION

For a bit more sweetness and texture, add the Crumble Topping (page 41).

It's Not a Galette, But. . .

If you're looking for a 5-minute treat, smash together 1 tablespoon each softened butter and the sour sugar mixture, slather over both sides of a slice of bread, then sear in a skillet over medium-high heat or pop in a 400°F (200°C) oven for a couple of minutes per side.

PRESERVED LEMON CURD

SERVES 6 TO 8

8 ounces (225 g) cream cheese, at room temperature

½ cup (160 g) lemon curd

2 tablespoons all-purpose flour

2 tablespoons powdered sugar

1 preserved lemon (about 60 g), very finely chopped, seeds removed; or 3 heaping tablespoons (60 g) preserved lemon paste (see Resources, page 228)

Kosher salt, if needed

Cooking spray or vegetable oil, for the pan

1 standard disk A Good Crust (page 27)

½ cup (70 g) crushed Biscoff cookies, gingersnaps, or Nilla wafers

1 large lemon, peeled, thinly sliced, and seeds removed (see Notes)

Egg wash: 1 large egg, beaten

2 teaspoons poppy seeds (optional)

Demerara or granulated sugar

Part lemon bar, part cheesecake, this is a cure for winter dessert woes. Here the citrus comes as a one-two-three punch: sliced lemon topping over a creamy filling with buttery lemon curd and finely chopped preserved lemon (it's salt-cured to render the citrus soft and tangy). Since there's no way to parbake galette crust (a well-known trick to avoid soggy bottoms for pies with custardy fillings), line the base with crushed Biscoff cookies. They soak up additional moisture without getting too soft, and add a layer of warm spice to each bite.

NOTES: *If you simply can't get into the idea of eating sliced lemon, swap in grapefruit or orange.*

Remember to lift the pan by its sides to avoid accidentally pushing out the removable bottom. To make your life easier, freeze the galette on a second sheet pan, tray, or cutting board before transferring it to the preheated sheet pan in the oven.

To unmold the galette, turn a medium bowl upside down and place the tart pan on top—the bowl will push up the removable bottom, separating the pan's wall while supporting the galette. Slide the galette onto a serving plate or cutting board (use a large offset or wide spatula to help if need be), then slice.

1 In a medium bowl, use a spatula to smash and stir the cream cheese and lemon curd together until the mixture is smooth. Fold in the flour, powdered sugar, and preserved lemon. (Alternatively, in a food processor, pulse the cream cheese and lemon curd until smooth, then pulse in the flour, sugar, and preserved lemon.) Taste and add a pinch of salt if needed (this will depend on how salty your preserved lemon is). Refrigerate this mixture.

Recipe continues

2 Preheat the oven to 425°F (220°C) with a rack positioned in the center. Place a sheet pan in the oven to preheat.

3 Grease a 9- or 10-inch (23 or 25 cm) tart pan with a removable bottom or springform pan with cooking spray. Roll the dough into a round and fit it into the pan using the Pan Method (page 36).

4 Sprinkle the cookie crumbs over the base of the crust, then spoon over the chilled filling and spread evenly. Layer the sliced lemon over the surface. Fold the edges of the crust over the filling, taking care to avoid it sinking in (if that does happen, just bake the galette anyway; it will be slightly less beautiful but no less tasty). Freeze the galette for 10 minutes (place the tart pan on another sheet pan to avoid touching the removable bottom).

5 Remove the galette from the freezer and brush the egg wash over the exposed crust. Sprinkle poppy seeds (if using) and demerara sugar over the crust.

6 Place the tart pan on the preheated sheet pan in the oven. Bake until the crust is starting to turn golden, 12 to 15 minutes. Reduce the oven temperature to 375°F (190°C) and continue to bake until the crust is deeply golden brown and the filling has puffed up (it will settle as it cools) and started to brown but is still a bit jiggly, another 30 to 35 minutes, rotating the sheet pan front to back halfway through.

7 Remove the galette from the oven and cool, uncovered, for 30 minutes or up to 2 hours before unmolding. Slice and serve.

Leftovers can be stored in an airtight container in the refrigerator for up to 24 hours.

BROWN-BUTTERED APPLES AND HONEY

Apples and honey remind me of Rosh Hashanah, the Jewish New Year celebration. Every fall when I was a kid, we'd gather around my grandparents' dining room table and cover wedges of tart, crisp apple with gobs of honey.

To make this memory into a galette, bathe apples in toasty browned butter tempered with honey and warm spices. The flavor profile and large-format size suggest this is destined to become a Thanksgiving favorite as well.

NOTE: *For an extra-crisp slab-galette crust, place a sheet pan in the oven as it preheats. Prepare the galette as written, freezing it on a second sheet pan. After brushing the galette with egg wash, remove the hot sheet pan from the oven and place it on a heatproof surface (like your stove). Bring the chilled galette nearby, carefully lift it by the parchment paper, and place it on the preheated sheet pan. Bake as directed.*

1 Roll out the dough and set it on a parchment-lined sheet pan using the Slab Method (page 36). Refrigerate on the sheet pan while you make the filling (it takes a while to arrange the apples so it's best for the dough to be extra-cold).

2 Melt the butter in a small skillet or saucepan over medium heat, stirring often to ensure it doesn't burn and continuing to cook until it foams and then browns and smells nutty, 3 to 5 minutes. Pour into a small bowl and immediately stir in the cinnamon (it will sizzle and smell fragrant). Let cool for a couple of minutes, then stir in the honey, vanilla, and kosher salt until smooth.

Recipe continues

SERVES 10 TO 12

1 XL disk A Good Crust (page 27)

4 tablespoons (60 g) unsalted butter, cut into small pieces

1½ teaspoons ground cinnamon or cardamom

2 tablespoons honey

1 teaspoon vanilla extract

1 teaspoon Diamond Crystal or ½ teaspoon Morton kosher salt

2 pounds (910 g) crisp, sweet apples (about 5 medium), such as Honeycrisp or Pink Lady

2 tablespoons cornstarch

1 tablespoon fresh lemon juice or apple cider vinegar

¼ cup (50 g) granulated or demerara sugar, plus more for sprinkling

Egg wash: 1 large egg, beaten

Flaky sea salt

½ cup (60 g) chopped toasted walnuts (optional), for serving

3 Slice the apples lengthwise off the core into 4 lobes. Slice each lobe lengthwise ⅛ inch (3 mm) thick. Place in a large bowl and toss with the cornstarch and lemon juice.

4 Preheat the oven to 425°F (220°C) with a rack positioned in the center.

5 Place the sheet pan with the chilled rolled-out dough on a work surface. Sprinkle the ¼ cup (50 g) sugar over the crust, leaving a 2-inch (5 cm) border. Fan out the apples over the sugar, overlapping as needed, in 3 or 4 rows (depending on the apple size). Brush the apples with the brown butter mixture. Fold the edges of the crust over the filling toward the center, overlapping and pleating as desired. Freeze the galette on the sheet pan for 15 minutes.

6 Remove the galette from the freezer and brush the egg wash over the exposed crust. Sprinkle more sugar over the crust.

7 Bake until the crust is starting to turn golden, 12 to 15 minutes. Reduce the oven temperature to 375°F (190°C) and continue to bake until the apples are tender and the crust is deeply golden brown, another 50 to 60 minutes, rotating the pan front to back halfway through.

8 Remove the galette from the oven and cool, uncovered, for at least 30 minutes and up to 8 hours.

9 Slice and serve, topped with flaky sea salt and the walnuts (if using).

Leftovers can be stored at room temperature, loosely covered, for up to 2 days. Reheat on a sheet pan in a 350°F (180°C) oven until warmed through, about 10 minutes.

CRUST VARIATION OPTIONS: Whole Wheat (page 39), Cornmeal (page 39)

SERVE WITH: Vanilla ice cream, Amaro Butterscotch (page 42), or Tangy Sweet Cream (page 42)

BLACK, BLUE, AND RED BERRIES

Blue and Black Berries

Gingery Cranberry Sauce

Jammy Grape

Roasted and Raw Berry
with Whole Lemon

Raspberry and Rose

Minty Blueberry-Chamomile

The word *berry* can refer to more fruit than you realize. Strangely, the botanical term excludes those commonly used in culinary vernacular, like raspberries, strawberries, and blackberries (they're actually called "aggregate fruit"). Cranberries, blueberries, and grapes, on the other hand, are "true berries." We can bake with them all, so no need to turn to the encyclopedia.

True or otherwise, berries bake up jammy-soft, holding on to just enough of their structure to create the most satisfying textural contrast with a galette's crisp crust. So when you get your hands on good ones, make the most of them. Hold a tiny raspberry and blueberry galette in each hand—no forks required. Pile a slice of cranberry sauce galette with a cloud of softly whipped cream to round out your Thanksgiving feast. And definitely leave some extra-ripe mixed berries out of the baked filling to finish one late-summer galette with a roasted-and-raw bang.

BLUE AND BLACK BERRIES

SERVES 6 TO 8

⅓ cup (65 g) sugar, plus more to taste and for sprinkling

2 teaspoons grated lemon zest

3 tablespoons (25 g) cornstarch

½ teaspoon Diamond Crystal or ¼ teaspoon Morton kosher salt, plus more to taste

1 pound (455 g) blackberries (about 3 cups)

6 ounces (170 g) blueberries (about 1 cup)

2 tablespoons black currant liqueur or crème de cassis (or 1 tablespoon blueberry jam mixed with 1 tablespoon fresh lemon juice)

1 standard disk A Good Crust (page 27)

Egg wash: 1 large egg, beaten

Maple syrup, for serving

CRUST VARIATION OPTIONS: Warm-Spice (page 40), Cocoa (page 39)

SERVE WITH: Vanilla ice cream or Maple Whip (page 42)

When I eat this galette, all I think about is *Walk Two Moons*, a heartbreakingly beautiful novel I loved dearly when I was a preteen. In one scene, the book's narrator, Sal, writes about her mother, who fills her mouth with blackberries from a nearby bush, then plants a kiss on a maple tree. While I don't harvest blackberries myself, nor do I have the closest relationship with the trees on my block, I *can* nestle berries into pastry and finish it with maple syrup.

1 Preheat the oven to 425°F (220°C) with a rack positioned in the center. Line a sheet pan with parchment paper.

2 In a large bowl, combine the sugar and zest and rub with your fingers until the sugar is slightly moistened and fragrant. Stir in the cornstarch and salt, then stir in the berries and liqueur. Taste a berry and season with another teaspoon of sugar and/or pinch of salt if the mixture seems a smidge bland.

3 Roll the dough into a round or rectangle and set it on the lined sheet pan using the Basic Method (page 34).

4 Leaving any excess liquid in the bowl, spoon the filling into the crust, leaving a 3-inch (7.5 cm) border. Fold the edges of the crust over the filling toward the center, overlapping and pleating as desired. Freeze the galette on the sheet pan for 10 minutes.

5 Remove the galette from the freezer and brush the egg wash over the exposed crust, then sprinkle with more sugar.

6 Bake until the crust is starting to turn golden, 12 to 15 minutes (if using a cocoa crust variation, look for the crust to darken slightly). Reduce the oven temperature to 375°F (190°C) and continue to bake until the fruit is bubbling and the crust is deeply golden brown, another 40 to 50 minutes, rotating the sheet pan front to back halfway through.

7 Remove the galette from the oven and cool, uncovered, for 25 minutes or up to 2 hours.

8 Drizzle the finished galette lightly with maple syrup. Slice and serve.

Leftovers can be stored at room temperature, loosely covered, for up to 2 days. Reheat on a sheet pan in a 350°F (180°C) oven until warmed through, about 10 minutes.

KEEPING BERRIES FRESH

Fresh berries don't have the longest lifespan. Ideally, they should be eaten or baked (or frozen) within a few days of purchasing, or you'll risk opening the container to find a mushy, moldy mess. There are, however, ways to push your luck. The moment you get home with your fruit, fill a large bowl with 3 cups (690 g) water and 1 cup (230 g) distilled white vinegar. Place the berries in a colander, lower it into the bowl, and let soak for 5 minutes. Pull up the berries by the colander, rinse with cold water, then gently spread onto a kitchen towel. Let them dry completely before storing in a dry towel–lined container in the fridge.

GINGERY CRANBERRY SAUCE

SERVES 6 TO 8

¾ cup (150 g) sugar, plus more for sprinkling

2 tablespoons grated grapefruit or orange zest

1 tablespoon finely grated fresh ginger

1 teaspoon Diamond Crystal or ½ teaspoon Morton kosher salt

1 pound (455 g) cranberries, fresh or frozen

¼ cup (60 g) fresh grapefruit or orange juice

2 tablespoons cornstarch

2 tablespoons bourbon or Grand Marnier (or more grapefruit or orange juice)

1 standard disk A Good Crust (page 27)

⅓ cup (55 g) candied ginger, roughly chopped (see Note)

Egg wash: 1 large egg, beaten

Fennel seeds (optional)

Cranberry sauce is often the underappreciated splotch of red on a Thanksgiving plate. Reimagined as a galette filling, it's the main event. You'll cook down the berries with sugar, citrus, and ginger until the mixture looks like, well, cranberry sauce. But this isn't just any cranberry sauce: Fold in candied ginger for pockets of chew and warm sweetness in the finished product. Top slices of this bracingly sweet-tart galette with freshly whipped unsweetened cream.

NOTE: *If you can't find candied ginger, swap in dried cranberries and up the fresh ginger to 2 tablespoons.*

1 In a medium saucepan, combine the sugar, zest, fresh ginger, and salt and rub together with your fingers until it smells fragrant. Stir in the cranberries and grapefruit juice. Cook over medium-high heat, stirring often with a spatula to ensure the mixture doesn't burn, until the cranberries have softened and the released liquid is bubbling, 5 to 8 minutes. Reduce the heat to medium and continue to boil, stirring occasionally, until the liquid has mostly reduced to a thicker consistency and the cranberries are starting to break down, another 5 to 8 minutes. Set up a large bowl of ice and water for an ice bath.

2 In a small bowl, stir together the cornstarch and bourbon until it forms a smooth slurry. Stir the slurry into the cranberry mixture and continue to cook, stirring often, until the mixture gets very thick and jammy, about 1 minute. You should be able to drag a spatula through the mixture and cleanly see the bottom of the pot as the filling slowly oozes over.

Recipe continues

CRUST VARIATION OPTIONS: Cornmeal (page 39), Cocoa (page 39)

SERVE WITH: Unsweetened whipped cream or Tangy Sweet Cream (page 42)

3 Scrape the mixture into a medium bowl set in the ice bath. Let cool to room temperature, about 30 minutes. If you're not making the galette right away, refrigerate in an airtight container for up to 1 week.

4 Preheat the oven to 425°F (220°C) with a rack positioned in the center. Line a sheet pan with parchment paper.

5 Roll the dough into a round or rectangle and set it on the lined sheet pan using the Basic Method (page 34).

6 Stir the candied ginger into the cranberry sauce. Spoon the cranberry sauce into the crust, leaving a 2-inch (5 cm) border. Fold the edges of the crust over the filling toward the center, overlapping and pleating as desired. Freeze the galette on the sheet pan for 10 minutes.

7 Remove the galette from the freezer and brush the egg wash over the exposed crust. Sprinkle fennel seeds (if using) over the crust, then sprinkle more sugar over the entire galette.

8 Bake until the crust is starting to turn golden, 12 to 15 minutes. Reduce the oven temperature to 375°F (190°C) and continue to bake until the crust is deeply golden brown, another 30 to 40 minutes, rotating the sheet pan front to back halfway through.

9 Remove the galette from the oven and cool, uncovered, for 25 minutes or up to 8 hours.

10 Slice and serve.

Leftovers can be stored at room temperature, loosely covered, for up to 2 days. Reheat on a sheet pan in a 350°F (180°C) oven until warmed through, about 10 minutes.

VARIATION

In spring, swap in strawberries and rhubarb for the cranberries. Use 8 ounces (225 g) of each, roughly chopped.

JAMMY GRAPE

We don't bake with grapes as often as we should. So often relegated to a jumbled fruit salad (where they end up lost in a sea of other flavors and textures), or worse yet, frozen into a flavorless, tooth-tingling "dessert," grapes deserve another look. Even the most average supermarket varieties—use black or red in a galette for their color—come alive when roasted with a bit of sugar and seasoning. They caramelize on the outside while the innards go jammy. Technically in season from summer to fall, the grapes available at the farmers market are truly special. They can be tart-skinned and fizzy inside, coated with cloudy (edible!) yeast, as small as blueberries, or oblong like doll-sized eggplants. All are welcome in this galette, so long as they're seedless. Finished with sesame (seeds and toasted oil), it tastes eerily like a PB&J sandwich.

1 Preheat the oven to 425°F (220°C) with a rack positioned in the center. Line a sheet pan with parchment paper.

2 In a large bowl, combine the grapes, sugar, cornstarch, port, rosemary (if using), and salt.

3 Roll the dough into a round or rectangle and set it on the lined sheet pan using the Basic Method (page 34).

4 Leaving any excess liquid in the bowl, spoon the filling into the crust, leaving a 3-inch (7.5 cm) border. Fold the edges of the crust over the filling toward the center, overlapping and pleating as desired. Freeze the galette on the sheet pan for 10 minutes.

Recipe continues

SERVES 6 TO 8

1¼ pounds (565 g) stemmed seedless black or red grapes (about 4 heaping cups), such as Black Corinth, Thomcord, and/or Flame

¼ cup (50 g) sugar, plus more for sprinkling

3 tablespoons (25 g) cornstarch

2 tablespoons tawny port, red vermouth, or balsamic vinegar

1 tablespoon chopped fresh rosemary or thyme leaves (optional)

½ teaspoon Diamond Crystal or ¼ teaspoon Morton kosher salt

1 standard disk A Good Crust (page 27)

Egg wash: 1 large egg, beaten

Sesame seeds

1 teaspoon toasted sesame oil (optional), for serving

CRUST VARIATION OPTIONS: Whole Wheat (page 39), Warm-Spice (page 40)

SERVE WITH: Nutty Drizzle (page 42) or Maple Whip (page 42)

5 Remove the galette from the freezer and brush the egg wash over the exposed crust. Sprinkle the sesame seeds and more sugar over the crust.

6 Bake until the crust is starting to turn golden, 12 to 15 minutes. Reduce the oven temperature to 375°F (190°C) and continue to bake until the fruit is bubbling and the crust is deeply golden brown, another 40 to 50 minutes, rotating the sheet pan front to back halfway through.

7 Remove the galette from the oven and cool, uncovered, for 25 minutes or up to 2 hours.

8 Slice and serve, drizzled with sesame oil (if using).

Leftovers can be stored at room temperature, loosely covered, for up to 2 days. Reheat on a sheet pan in a 350°F (180°C) oven until warmed through, about 10 minutes.

ROASTED AND RAW BERRY
WITH WHOLE LEMON

SERVES 6 TO 8

⅓ cup (65 g) plus 2 tablespoons sugar

3 tablespoons (25 g) cornstarch

2 teaspoons ground cardamom or ginger

½ teaspoon Diamond Crystal or ¼ teaspoon Morton kosher salt, plus more to taste

2 pounds (910 g) mixed berries (about 6¼ cups), such as blueberries, raspberries, blackberries, and quartered strawberries (any one or any mixture works)

½ large (30 g) lemon, thickly sliced, seeds removed, very finely chopped (about 3 tablespoons)

Cooking spray or vegetable oil, for the pan

1 standard disk A Good Crust (page 27)

Egg wash: 1 large egg, beaten

If you arrive at the farmers market at the start of berry season and go wild with excitement, purchasing a pint or two at each stall, make this with your haul. Like with most fruit galettes, you'll start by mixing together a filling, including any underripe or slightly squashed specimens. But then you'll break decorum: Save the ripest, most perfectly shaped berries for spooning raw over the baked pastry.

To further set this one apart from other mixed-berry desserts on the table, finely chop half a lemon—yes, pith, peel, and flesh—into a paste to stir into the filling and topping. It adds a welcome bittersweet zing to the sweet berries (and the pith offers a smidge of additional pectin, which helps set the juicy filling).

1 Preheat the oven to 425°F (220°C) with a rack positioned in the center. Place a sheet pan in the oven to preheat.

2 In a large bowl, whisk together ⅓ cup (65 g) of the sugar, the cornstarch, cardamom, and salt. Stir in 4½ cups (about 680 g) of the berries and 2 tablespoons of the chopped lemon. Depending on how ripe your berries are, this mixture may be a bit dry (don't worry; it will get plenty jammy in the oven).

3 Grease a 9- or 10-inch (23 or 25 cm) cast-iron skillet, pie plate, or cake pan with cooking spray. Roll the dough into a round and fit it into the pan using the Pan Method (page 36).

Recipe continues

SPECIAL EQUIPMENT:
9- or 10-inch (23 or 25 cm) cast-iron skillet, metal or ceramic pie plate, or cake pan

CRUST VARIATION OPTION: Cornmeal (page 39)

SERVE WITH: Vanilla ice cream or Maple Whip (page 42)

4 Leaving any excess liquid in the bowl, spoon the filling into the crust. Fold the edges of the crust over the filling toward the center, overlapping and pleating as desired. Freeze the galette for 10 minutes.

5 Remove the galette from the freezer and brush the egg wash over the exposed crust.

6 Place the skillet on the preheated sheet pan in the oven. Bake until the crust is starting to turn golden, 12 to 15 minutes. Reduce the oven temperature to 375°F (190°C) and continue to bake until the fruit is bubbling and the crust is deeply golden brown, another 45 to 55 minutes, rotating the sheet pan front to back halfway through.

7 Remove the galette from the oven and cool, uncovered, for 30 minutes or up to 8 hours.

8 At least 30 minutes and up to 8 hours before serving, in a medium bowl, combine the remaining berries, 1 tablespoon chopped lemon, and 2 tablespoons sugar. Season with a pinch or two of salt to taste. Let the berries macerate in the refrigerator until you're ready to serve.

9 Top the galette with the fresh berry mixture (use as much or as little of the juices as you'd like). Slice and serve.

Best eaten day-of. With topping, leftovers can be stored in an airtight container in the refrigerator for up to 2 days.

WHEN AND HOW TO GALETTE WITH FROZEN FRUIT

Frozen fruit is a miracle. Preserving fruit at peak ripeness and coming back to it months later to find it virtually unchanged suggests some kind of witchcraft is at play. While all fruit can technically be frozen, the process will alter the cell walls a bit as the water inside turns into ice. Once frozen, a fruit's texture will always thaw softer than the fresh version. Some types of fruit take better to freezing than others* when it comes to baking into galettes, and each should be prepared a bit differently.

To freeze your own fruit, wash and dry the fruit as you would normally. Remove and discard any stems or leaves. For stone fruit, pit and slice into ½-inch (13 mm) wedges. For figs, halve or quarter if large. Leave most berries whole; halve large strawberries. Line a sheet pan with parchment paper and arrange the fruit without pieces touching (work in batches as needed). Freeze until the fruit is solid, about 3 hours, then transfer to airtight containers or ziplock bags. Depending on the quality of your freezer, the frozen fruit should last 6 to 8 months without freezer burn.

It's not necessary to thaw the fruit or add additional thickener before using it in the filling (unless a recipe specifically says so). But thawed or not, the fruit will have a slightly softer texture when baked, so in order to ensure the galette is crisp all the way though, it will likely need an extra 5 to 10 minutes in the oven.

*Baked from frozen (or thawed) in galettes, strawberries, raspberries, and rhubarb go overly soft, running the risk of a soggy-bottomed crust. I prefer to skip these except for in tiny galettes, or when I'm only using a cup or so of frozen fruit along with fresh. They do, however, work if you're making a spreadable precooked filling—say, swapping in one of the aforementioned fruits for the Sour Cherry and Campari (page 61) or Gingery Cranberry Sauce (page 90) galettes.

RASPBERRY AND ROSE

(Pictured on page 65)

**MAKES 8 SMALL
GALETTES**

1 XL disk A Good Crust
(page 27)

¼ cup (50 g) sugar, plus more
for sprinkling

3 tablespoons (25 g) cornstarch

2 tablespoons raspberry jam

1 tablespoon apple cider
vinegar or fresh lemon juice

¾ teaspoon rose water

½ teaspoon Diamond Crystal
or ¼ teaspoon Morton
kosher salt

1¼ pounds (565 g) raspberries
(about 4 cups)

Egg wash: 1 large egg, beaten

**CRUST VARIATION
OPTIONS:** Buckwheat
(page 39), Cocoa (page 39)

SERVE WITH: Vanilla ice
cream or Tangy Sweet Cream
(page 42)

Raspberry and rose water is one of those flavor
combinations that tastes as good as it sounds. And in
a handheld galette, what could possibly be sweeter?
Keep your eye out for the most vibrantly colored fruit,
which boasts the most flavor. Of course, if you can
only find pale, out-of-season berries, don't fret: A good
dollop of raspberry jam in the filling makes up for any
blandness, or you can pivot to frozen. These galettes
are basically hand pies, but if you don't mind a fork-and-
knife situation, top with a dollop of something sweet and
creamy.

NOTE: *If you want to use frozen (unthawed) raspberries
instead of fresh, it's okay to use a bit less of the filling,
as the larger and firmer berries sometimes have a hard
time fitting into the small galette crusts.*

1 Preheat the oven to 375°F (190°C) with racks positioned in
the upper and lower thirds.

2 Roll out 8 rounds of dough using the Tiny Method (page 36).
Refrigerate on a plate (it's okay if they overlap) while you make
the filling.

3 In a large bowl, stir together the sugar, cornstarch, jam,
vinegar, rose water, and salt. Fold in the raspberries.

4 Line a sheet pan with parchment paper. Place one small
dough round on the lined pan. Pile the center with about
⅓ cup (85 g) of the raspberry mixture, leaving at least a 2-inch
(5 cm) border. Brush the border around the filling with some
egg wash. Fold and pleat the edges of the crust toward the
center, pressing gently to adhere, making sure to overlap the

crust and almost entirely cover the filling (it will spread as it bakes). Repeat with the remaining 7 dough rounds. Freeze the galettes on the sheet pan for 15 minutes.

5 Line a second sheet pan with parchment paper. Remove the galettes from the freezer and carefully transfer half the galettes to the second pan, spacing apart evenly. In both pans, brush more egg wash over the exposed crusts. Sprinkle more sugar over each galette.

6 Bake until the crusts are deeply golden brown and the filling is bubbling, 50 to 60 minutes, switching racks and rotating the sheet pans front to back halfway through. If any of the edges unfold during the first half of baking, you can use a butter knife to gently refold them when rotating the pans.

7 Remove the galettes from the oven and cool, uncovered, for 15 minutes or up to 2 hours.

Leftovers can be stored at room temperature, loosely covered, for up to 2 days. Reheat on a sheet pan in a 350°F (180°C) oven until warmed through, about 10 minutes.

VARIATIONS

If you're not into floral flavor, skip the rose water and use 2 teaspoons vanilla extract or ½ teaspoon orange blossom water.

In spring, swap in fresh strawberries and rhubarb for the raspberries. Use 10 ounces (285 g) of each, roughly chopped.

MINTY BLUEBERRY-CHAMOMILE

(Pictured on page 65)

MAKES 8 SMALL GALETTES

1 XL disk A Good Crust (page 27)

⅓ cup (65 g) sugar, plus more for sprinkling

3 tablespoons (8 g) chamomile tea leaves

1 tablespoon peppermint tea leaves

1¼ pounds (565 g) small blueberries (about 4 cups), fresh or frozen (not thawed)

3 tablespoons (25 g) cornstarch

1 tablespoon apple cider vinegar

½ teaspoon Diamond Crystal or ¼ teaspoon Morton kosher salt, plus more to taste

Egg wash: 1 large egg, beaten

Honey (optional), for serving

CRUST VARIATION OPTIONS: Whole Wheat (page 39), Cornmeal (page 39)

SERVE WITH: Vanilla ice cream or Maple Whip (page 42)

If you have yet to use herbal tea leaves such as mint or chamomile in your baking, there's no time like the present. A high-quality loose tea will be the most potent with earthy roasted blueberries, but as long as they're relatively fresh, feel free to snip open tea bags you have in the pantry. Use small fresh or frozen blueberries here (if labeled "wild" they're the right size), as larger ones tend to be harder to tuck into the small crusts. If you can only find bulbous berries, use your fingers to gently crush some of them as you make the filling, or instead make one big galette (see Variations).

1 Preheat the oven to 375°F (190°C) with racks positioned in the upper and lower thirds.

2 Roll out 8 rounds of dough using the Tiny Method (page 36). Refrigerate on a plate (it's okay if they overlap) while you make the filling.

3 In a large bowl, combine the sugar and the chamomile and peppermint tea leaves. Use your fingers to rub them together, breaking up the tea a bit, until the mixture is fragrant. Stir in the blueberries, cornstarch, vinegar, and salt (this mixture may be on the dry side, especially if using fresh berries).

4 Line a sheet pan with parchment paper. Place one small dough round on the lined pan. Pile the center with about ⅓ cup (85 g) of the blueberry mixture, leaving at least a 2-inch (5 cm) border. Brush the border around the filling with some egg wash. Fold and pleat the edges of the crust toward the center, pressing gently to adhere, making sure to overlap the crust and almost entirely cover the filling (it will spread as it bakes). Repeat with the remaining 7 dough rounds. Freeze the galettes on the sheet pan for 15 minutes.

5 Line a second sheet pan with parchment paper. Remove the galettes from the freezer and carefully transfer half the galettes to the second pan, spacing apart evenly. In both pans, brush more egg wash over the exposed crusts. Sprinkle more sugar over each galette.

6 Bake until the crusts are deeply golden brown and the filling is bubbling, 50 to 60 minutes, switching racks and rotating the sheet pans front to back halfway through. If any of the edges unfold during the first half of baking, you can use a butter knife to gently refold them when rotating the pans.

7 Remove the galettes from the oven and cool, uncovered, for 15 minutes or up to 2 hours.

8 If desired, drizzle the filling of each galette with honey before serving.

Leftovers can be stored at room temperature, loosely covered, for up to 2 days. Reheat on a sheet pan in a 350°F (180°C) oven until warmed through, about 10 minutes.

VARIATIONS

For a more tea-forward version, use 2 tablespoons total of chai (black or rooibos varieties will work) or Earl Grey tea leaves, both of which are stronger in flavor than the mint and chamomile.

To make one big galette: Use 1 standard disk A Good Crust rolled into a round or rectangle and set it on the lined sheet pan (using the Basic Method, page 34). Pour all the filling into the crust, leaving a 3-inch (7.5 cm) border. Fold the edges of the crust over the filling toward the center, overlapping and pleating as desired. Freeze the galette on the sheet pan for 10 minutes. Bake at 425°F (220°C) for 12 to 15 minutes, then reduce the heat to 375°F (190°C) and continue to bake until the crust is deeply golden brown and the filling is bubbling, another 40 to 50 minutes, rotating the sheet pan front to back halfway through. Cool and serve as directed.

CHOCOLATE AND OTHER SWEET THINGS

Some sweet galettes don't need much, if any, produce. In fact, this chapter actually houses some of my favorite recipes—I'll always opt for a chocolate- or nut-based dessert over those composed of out-of-season baked fruit. Most of these galettes can be made any time of year, as they rely primarily on packaged or shelf-stable baking ingredients. You'll crumble halva and dot with Maraschino cherries. You'll dollop globs of miso, Nutella, frangipane, and pastry cream. Fresh fruit fans: Don't move on. Pineapple, figs, strawberries, banana, and your choice of persimmon or rhubarb guest star in these pages.

Compared with all-fruit galettes, which can last a few days but are best eaten immediately, nut-based galettes have a longer postbake life. In fact, they're the only galette recipes I actually prefer on day two to fresh from the oven—especially if they've sat overnight in the fridge. Think of the difference between a slice of cold cake (fudgy-firm) and a warm one (crumbly-moist). Biting into one of these cold galettes reminds me of *tandsmør*, the Danish term for butter spread so thickly on bread that you leave teeth marks when you take a bite.

HANDHELD CHOCOLATE-HAZELNUT

MAKES 8 SMALL GALETTES

1 XL disk A Good Crust (page 27)

3 large eggs

1¼ cups (370 g) sweetened chocolate-hazelnut spread, such as Nutella

1½ teaspoons Diamond Crystal or ¾ teaspoon Morton kosher salt

4 to 6 stemmed and sliced strawberries, 1 sliced banana, or a mix (optional)

Demerara or granulated sugar

Flaky sea salt

CRUST VARIATION OPTIONS: Buckwheat (page 39), Warm-Spice (page 40)

SERVE WITH: A good cappuccino

Anyone who grew up loving Nutella crepes will be equally delighted with these little galettes. The filling couldn't be simpler: chocolate-hazelnut spread, eggs, and salt, which bakes into a texture somewhere between a brownie and fudge. You don't *have* to add sliced strawberries or bananas, but if the mention of those crepes unlocks a core memory, you know the fruit makes the dish. (You could dust the baked pastries with powdered sugar, à la crepes, but I prefer a sprinkle of flaky sea salt over the top.)

1 Preheat the oven to 375°F (190°C) with racks positioned in the upper and lower thirds.

2 Roll out 8 dough rounds using the Tiny Method (page 36). Refrigerate on a plate (it's okay if they overlap) while you make the filling.

3 In a medium bowl, use a fork or whisk to beat 2 of the eggs, then beat in the chocolate-hazelnut spread and kosher salt (it will look clumpy and separated at first but will come together as you keep beating).

4 Line a sheet pan with parchment paper. Place one small dough round on the lined pan. Spoon 2 heaping tablespoons (55 g) chocolate-hazelnut mixture into the center, leaving at least a 2-inch (5 cm) border. If using, arrange a few strawberry or banana slices over the filling. Repeat with the remaining 7 dough rounds.

5 In a small bowl, beat the remaining egg to make an egg wash. Working with one galette at a time, brush the border around the filling with some egg wash. Fold and pleat the edges of the crust toward the center, pressing gently to adhere, making sure to overlap the crust and almost entirely cover the filling (it will spread as it bakes). Freeze the galettes on the sheet pan for 20 minutes.

6 Line a second sheet pan with parchment paper. Remove the galettes from the freezer and carefully transfer half the galettes to the second pan, spacing apart evenly. In both pans, brush more egg wash over the exposed crusts. Sprinkle sugar over the galettes.

7 Bake until the crusts are deeply golden brown, 30 to 40 minutes, switching racks and rotating the sheet pans front to back halfway through. If any of the edges unfold during the first half of baking, you can use a butter knife to gently refold them when rotating the pans. The filling should be darkened, puffed, and starting to crack in spots (sort of like a brownie).

8 Remove the galettes from the oven and sprinkle with some flaky sea salt. Cool, uncovered, for 15 minutes or up to 8 hours.

Leftovers can be stored in an airtight container in the refrigerator for up to 2 days (3 days without fruit). Reheat if desired (but they're pretty great cold) on a sheet pan in a 350°F (180°C) oven until warmed through, about 10 minutes.

FIGGY MISO

¼ cup (85 g) fig jam

2 tablespoons white miso

1¼ pounds (565 g) fresh figs, such as Black Mission or Adriatic (see Note), halved (or quartered if larger than 2 inches/5 cm)

2 tablespoons sugar, plus more for sprinkling

1 tablespoon Cynar, fresh lemon juice, or balsamic vinegar

1 standard disk A Good Crust (page 27)

Egg wash: 1 large egg, beaten

2 tablespoons sliced almonds or crushed blanched hazelnuts (optional)

Flaky sea salt

Extra-virgin olive oil, for serving

CRUST VARIATION OPTIONS: Whole Wheat (page 39), Buckwheat (page 39)

SERVE WITH: Soft, tangy cheese, such as chèvre, Brie, or blue

There's no better partner to sugary-sweet figs than salty miso. Mixed with jam and spread on the bottom of a galette, the earthy paste tempers sweetness and enhances the fruit's more nuanced flavors. For the rest of the filling, toss fresh figs in the bittersweet liqueur Cynar. Named for artichokes, one of its main ingredients, the aperitivo (or digestivo, depending on whom you ask) is far more herbal than other amari. Instead of dousing with cream (whipped or ice), try this galette alongside globs of soft cheese.

NOTE: *Fresh figs don't have an especially long season. If there are none to be found, swap in ½-inch (13 mm) wedges of peach, plum, pear, or apple.*

1 Preheat the oven to 425°F (220°C) with a rack positioned in the center. Line a sheet pan with parchment paper.

2 Place the jam in a small bowl and stir and smash with a spatula to loosen. Use the spatula to smash and stir in the miso 1 tablespoon at a time until smooth. In a medium bowl, toss the figs with sugar and Cynar.

3 Roll the dough into a rectangle or round and set it on the lined sheet pan using the Basic Method (page 34).

4 Spoon the jam filling into the crust, leaving a 2-inch (5 cm) border. Arrange the figs over the filling, cut-side up, then spoon any excess liquid in the bowl over the top.

5 Fold the edges of the crust over the filling toward the center to make a rectangle, overlapping and pleating as desired. Freeze the galette on the sheet pan for 10 minutes.

Recipe continues

6 Remove the galette from the freezer and brush the egg wash over the exposed crust. Sprinkle the almonds (if using) and more sugar over the crust.

7 Bake until the crust is starting to turn golden, 12 to 15 minutes. Reduce the oven temperature to 375°F (190°C) and continue to bake until the figs are tender and the crust is deeply golden brown, another 35 to 40 minutes, rotating the sheet pan front to back halfway through.

8 Remove the galette from the oven and sprinkle with some flaky sea salt. Cool, uncovered, for 30 minutes or up to 8 hours. Drizzle with extra-virgin olive oil, then slice and serve.

Leftovers can be stored at room temperature, loosely covered, for up to 2 days. Reheat on a sheet pan in a 350°F (180°C) oven until warmed through, about 10 minutes.

NOT QUITE GALETTE DES ROIS

Visit France in January and nearly every bakery will be packed with galettes des rois, two puff-pastry rounds filled with frangipane. (The translation complicates things, but don't confuse it with king cake, the colorfully frosted or dried fruit–adorned enriched dough ring also intended for Epiphany celebrations.) Here the French pastry is reinterpreted as a galette using A Good Crust and is—duh!—baked open-faced. Fernet-spiked frangipane filling is my dream spread, but feel free to use your favorite amaro, or even bourbon or dark rum. Stick an almond into the filling as an homage to the "fève," or ceramic figurine, which was historically included in the pastry. Where a galette des rois is scored to make a swirled top crust, this galette gets baked in a tart pan, its fluted sides an ode to the pattern.

NOTES: *Remember to lift the pan by its sides to avoid accidentally pushing out the removable bottom. To make your life easier, freeze the galette on a second sheet pan, tray, or cutting board before transferring it to the preheated sheet pan in the oven.*

To unmold the galette, turn a medium bowl upside down and place the tart pan on top—the bowl will push up the removable bottom, separating the pan's wall while supporting the galette. Slide the galette onto a serving plate or cutting board (use a large offset or wide spatula to help if need be), then slice.

Recipe continues

SERVES 6 TO 8

1 cup (115 g) superfine blanched almond flour

¾ cup (150 g) sugar

2 tablespoons all-purpose flour

1 teaspoon Diamond Crystal or ½ teaspoon Morton kosher salt

3 tablespoons (45 g) unsalted butter, at room temperature

3 large eggs

1 tablespoon Fernet or preferred amaro, dark rum, or bourbon (or 2 teaspoons vanilla extract)

¼ teaspoon almond extract

Cooking spray or vegetable oil, for the pan

1 standard disk A Good Crust (page 27)

1 raw almond (optional)

Flaky sea salt

SPECIAL EQUIPMENT:
9- or 10-inch (23 or 25 cm) tart pan with a removable bottom or springform pan

CRUST VARIATION OPTIONS: Buckwheat (page 39), Warm-Spice (page 40)

1 Preheat the oven to 425°F (220°C) with a rack positioned in the center. Place a sheet pan in the oven to preheat.

2 In a medium bowl, whisk together the almond flour, sugar, all-purpose flour, and kosher salt. In another medium bowl, use a spatula to smash the butter until soft and smooth, then whisk in 2 of the eggs, the amaro, and almond extract until smooth. Fold the almond mixture into the butter mixture until smooth. (Alternatively, pulse together the dry ingredients in a food processor, then pulse in the wet ingredients until smooth.) Refrigerate the frangipane in the bowl while rolling out the crust, or in an airtight container for up to 1 week.

3 Grease a 9- or 10-inch (23 or 25 cm) tart pan with a removable bottom or springform pan with cooking spray. Roll the dough into a round and fit it into the pan using the Pan Method (page 36).

4 Spoon the frangipane into the crust. If using, press the raw almond into the filling close to an edge of the pan. Fold the edges of the crust over the filling toward the center, overlapping and pleating as desired (make sure to cover the almond!). Freeze the galette for 10 minutes (place the tart pan on another sheet pan to avoid touching the removable bottom).

5 In a small bowl, beat the remaining egg to make an egg wash. Remove the galette from the freezer and brush the exposed crust with the egg wash.

6 Place the tart pan on the preheated sheet pan in the oven. Bake until the crust is starting to turn golden, 12 to 15 minutes. Reduce the oven temperature to 375°F (190°C) and continue to bake until the crust is deeply golden brown and the filling has puffed, another 30 to 40 minutes, rotating the sheet pan front to back halfway through. If the exposed filling starts to look deeply golden before 30 minutes, gently tent the filling with foil and continue baking.

Recipe continues

7 Remove the galette from the oven and sprinkle with some flaky sea salt. Cool, uncovered, for 30 minutes or up to 8 hours before unmolding. Slice and serve.

Leftovers can be stored in an airtight container in the refrigerator or at room temperature for up to 3 days. Reheat if desired (but it's pretty great cold) on a sheet pan in a 350°F (180°C) oven until warmed through, about 10 minutes.

It's Not a Galette, But...

For a halfway-homemade treat, slice open store-bought croissants and slather the inside of each with 1 tablespoon of the frangipane filling. Sandwich the croissant tops over the filled halves, then spread the tops with another tablespoon of frangipane. Sprinkle with flaky salt and sliced almonds if you'd like. Place on a parchment-lined sheet pan and bake at 375°F (190°C) until golden, 12 to 15 minutes.

ALMOST CANNOLI

I grew up devouring pastries from Italian bakeries around northern New Jersey. Cannoli and sfogliatelle in particular made such an impression that I cannot pass an establishment that makes either without stopping. (Sweet ricotta filling, shatteringly crisp dough; need I say more?) Both require complex technique—one dough deep-fried around a special tube; the other stretched feet-long and paper-thin—so actually making these treats is best left to the professionals. But a galette-inspired variation? That's a snap to do at home.

NOTE: *Candied orange peel can be tricky to find at supermarkets but is easy to source online as well as to make yourself. If you prefer to DIY, see page 121 for a quick method.*

1 Heat the milk in a medium saucepan over medium-low heat until it starts to steam and bubble at the edges, 5 to 7 minutes. In a medium bowl, whisk together the sugar, cornstarch, and salt. Whisk in the egg yolks until very smooth. Set up a large bowl of ice and water for an ice bath.

2 Whisking constantly, very slowly pour about 1 cup (230 g) of the hot milk into the sugar mixture until the mixture is completely smooth (add it too fast and you'll risk scrambling the eggs). Pour the sugar-milk mixture into the remaining milk in the saucepan.

3 Return the saucepan to medium-low heat and continue to cook, whisking constantly, until the mixture has thickened to the consistency of very thick pudding, 4 to 5 minutes. It will seem like nothing is happening at first, then thicken—continue to cook until it is thick enough to drag a spatula through the

MAKES 8 SMALL GALETTES

2½ cups (575 g) whole milk

½ cup (100 g) sugar, plus more for sprinkling

6 tablespoons (45 g) cornstarch

1½ teaspoons Diamond Crystal or ¾ teaspoon Morton kosher salt

8 large egg yolks

1 XL disk A Good Crust (page 27)

Scant 1 cup (225 g) whole-milk ricotta cheese

⅓ cup (55 g) chopped Quick-Candied Orange Peel (recipe follows), plus more for serving

1 tablespoon Grand Marnier (or 1 teaspoon orange blossom water plus 1 teaspoon honey)

Egg wash: 1 large egg, beaten

¼ cup (45 g) finely chopped bittersweet chocolate or mini chocolate chips

¼ cup (30 g) finely chopped salted roasted pistachios

CRUST VARIATION OPTION: Cocoa (page 39)

SERVE WITH: Strong espresso

mixture and cleanly see the bottom of the pot as the mixture very slowly fills the gap. Immediately remove from the heat and scrape into a clean medium bowl set in the ice bath. Let cool to room temperature, about 30 minutes. Cover and refrigerate until the mixture is completely chilled, at least 2 hours and up to 2 days.

4 When you're ready to bake, roll out 8 rounds of dough using the Tiny Method (page 36). Refrigerate on a plate (it's okay if they overlap) while you finish the filling.

5 Remove the chilled milk mixture from the refrigerator and use a fork or whisk to stir until smooth. Fold in the ricotta, candied orange peel, and Grand Marnier until combined.

6 Preheat the oven to 375°F (190°C) with racks positioned in the upper and lower thirds.

7 Line a sheet pan with parchment paper. Place one dough round on the lined pan. Spoon a heaping ⅓ cup (100 g) of the ricotta cream into the center, leaving at least a 2-inch (5 cm) border. Brush the border around the filling with some egg wash. Fold and pleat the edges of the crust toward the center, pressing gently to adhere, making sure to overlap the crust and almost entirely cover the filling (it will spread as it bakes). Repeat with the remaining 7 dough rounds (snack on any leftover filling). Freeze the galettes on the sheet pan for 15 minutes.

8 Line a second sheet pan with parchment paper. Remove the galettes from the freezer and carefully transfer half the galettes to the second pan, spacing apart evenly. In both pans, brush more egg wash over the exposed crusts. Sprinkle more sugar over each galette.

9 Bake until the crusts are deeply golden brown and the filling is set and starting to take on color in spots, 40 to 50 minutes, switching racks and rotating the sheet pans front to back halfway through. If any of the edges unfold during the first half of baking, you can use a butter knife to gently refold them when rotating the pans.

Recipe continues

10 Remove the galettes from the oven and cool, uncovered, for 15 minutes or up to 2 hours.

11 Sprinkle the center of each with chocolate and pistachios before serving.

Best eaten day-of. Leftovers can be stored in the refrigerator, loosely covered, for 24 hours.

It's Not a Galette, But. . .

Sans galette, the ricotta filling is excellent between the layers of a cake, smeared onto pancakes, or eaten straight from a bowl like pudding.

VARIATION

For a galette that's slightly less Italian pastry–inspired, omit the candied orange peel (from the filling and topping) and chocolate, and top each baked galette with a spoonful of chopped fresh fruit or berries. Sprinkle with chopped pistachios and/or flaky sea salt if you'd like.

Quick-Candied Orange Peel

Candying your own citrus peel allows you the freedom to try grapefruit, lemon, and less-common orange varieties. Fold extras into cookie dough and baked granola, or snack on it like any other candy.

1 Slice the top and bottom off the oranges, then rest on one flat edge. Slice the peel (with pith) off the oranges, following the curve of the fruit. Reserve the flesh for another use (such as the Creamy Pistachio and Citrus galette, page 70). Slice the peel into strips ¼ inch (6 mm) wide.

2 In a medium saucepan, combine 1 cup (200 g) of the sugar and 1 cup (230 g) water and whisk together until the sugar is dissolved. Add the orange peel strips. Bring the mixture to a boil over medium-high heat and cook, stirring occasionally, until the liquid starts to thicken. Reduce the heat to medium-low and continue to cook until the liquid becomes a thick syrup about the consistency of maple syrup, about 20 minutes. Remove from the heat.

3 Use a slotted spoon to transfer the orange peels to a wire rack (placed over a sheet pan to catch drips). Try to separate the peels as best you can so they don't touch and let cool for at least 30 minutes and up to overnight while the excess syrup drips off.

4 Pour the remaining ¼ cup (50 g) sugar into a small bowl. Working with a few pieces at a time, toss the candied peels in the sugar, making sure to coat each one well enough so they no longer stick to each other. Repeat with the remaining peels, adding more sugar to the bowl as needed. Store the candied orange peel in an airtight container in the refrigerator for up to 1 month. Leftover syrup can be used as a swap for simple syrup—refrigerate in an airtight container for up to 1 month.

MAKES ABOUT 1 CUP (170 G)

2 medium oranges (or 1 large/ 2 small grapefruits, or 3 lemons)

1¼ cups (250 g) sugar, plus more as needed

RHUBARB (OR PERSIMMON!) WITH HALVA

SERVES 6 TO 8

1¼ pounds (565 g) rhubarb stalks, any leaves removed; or 3 to 4 Fuyu persimmons, stemmed

3 to 5 tablespoons (40 to 60 g) sugar, plus more for sprinkling

2 teaspoons grated grapefruit or lemon zest

1 tablespoon cornstarch

1 tablespoon Campari or Aperol (or fresh grapefruit or lemon juice)

½ teaspoon Diamond Crystal or ¼ teaspoon Morton kosher salt

1 standard disk A Good Crust (page 27)

Heaping ½ cup (80 g) crumbled halva (see Notes)

Egg wash: 1 large egg, beaten

Sesame seeds

CRUST VARIATION OPTIONS: Cocoa (page 39), Buckwheat (page 39)

SERVE WITH: Vanilla ice cream or Tangy Sweet Cream (page 42)

A choose-your-own-adventure of sorts: Use tart rhubarb in spring and summer and honey-sweet persimmon in fall and winter. Both fruits pop up at the farmers market and some grocery stores for just a few months a year, making them all the more special. That said, if you're in a pinch and can't find specialty fruit, swap in peach, plum, pear, or apple wedges (follow the instructions for persimmons). Crumble halva, a fudgy sesame confection, into the crust for a nutty-sweet base underneath tender roasted fruit.

NOTES: *Scoring rhubarb helps keep the stalks from curling too much or splitting in a weird way in the oven, which is especially helpful if you'd like to tile the batons into a uniform pattern. Gently run a knife vertically down each stalk a few times, not piercing all the way through, then slice as desired.*

Halva can be made with just tahini and sugar but can also be swirled with other ingredients like chopped nuts or chocolate. Any variety should work here. It is available at certain supermarkets and specialty stores; see Resources (page 228). If you can't find it, use Crumble Topping (page 41) with 1 tablespoon tahini mixed in.

1 **If using rhubarb:** Lightly score the stalks lengthwise (see Notes), then slice the stalks into batons no wider than ½ inch (13 mm) thick and between 2 and 5 inches (5 and 12.5 cm) long. **If using persimmons (or another fruit):** Slice the fruit (no need to peel) into wedges ½ inch (13 mm) thick.

Recipe continues

2 In a large bowl, combine the sugar (if using rhubarb, use 5 tablespoons/60 g; persimmons, use 3 tablespoons/40 g) and zest and rub with your fingers until the sugar is slightly moistened and fragrant. Stir in the cornstarch, Campari, and salt (the mixture will be thick). Toss in the sliced fruit to coat in the sugar-zest mixture.

3 Preheat the oven to 425°F (220°C) with a rack positioned in the center. Line a sheet pan with parchment paper.

4 Roll the dough into a round or rectangle and set it on the lined sheet pan using the Basic Method (page 34).

5 Scatter the halva over the crust, leaving a 3-inch (7.5 cm) border. Arrange the fruit mixture in whatever way brings you joy. Fold the edges of the crust over the filling toward the center, overlapping and pleating as desired. Freeze the galette on the sheet pan for 10 minutes.

6 Remove the galette from the freezer and brush the egg wash over the exposed crust. Sprinkle sesame seeds and more sugar over the crust (if using rhubarb, sprinkle 2 tablespoons of sugar over the entire galette).

7 Bake until the crust is starting to turn golden, 12 to 15 minutes (if using a cocoa crust variation, look for the crust to darken slightly). Reduce the oven temperature to 375°F (190°C) and continue to bake until the filling has puffed up and the crust is deeply golden brown, another 30 to 40 minutes, rotating the sheet pan front to back halfway through.

8 Remove the galette from the oven and cool, uncovered, for 30 minutes or up to 8 hours (the filling will settle, and the halva will be very gooey when warm and firm up as it cools). Slice and serve.

Leftovers can be stored in an airtight container at room temperature for up to 2 days. Reheat on a sheet pan in a 350°F (180°C) oven until warmed through, about 10 minutes.

COCOA AND TOASTED PECAN

This is a galette for the people who aren't into fruit desserts. This is also a galette for the people who just can't find a pecan pie they love. And this is definitely a galette for the people who forgo cakes and pies on the dessert table in favor of a brownie or blondie. Rum-spiked pecan (or walnut) frangipane bakes up firm but chewy thanks to the addition of brown sugar. Enfold in a cocoa or buckwheat crust and stud the top with bittersweet chocolate for a bake that will change the way you think about galettes. One bite, and you'll agree: Maybe a perfect galette actually doesn't—*gasp*—need fruit at all.

NOTE: *For a filling that's more reminiscent of a blondie than a brownie, omit the cocoa powder in the frangipane and use 3 tablespoons (25 g) flour total.*

1 Preheat the oven to 350°F (180°C) with a rack positioned in the center.

2 Spread the nuts on a sheet pan and toast until just barely starting to become fragrant (they should not darken or toast completely), about 5 minutes. Transfer to a plate and let cool completely, about 20 minutes. The lightly toasted nuts can be stored in an airtight container in the refrigerator but are best used within 2 months.

3 In a food processor, combine 1 cup plus 3 tablespoons (145 g) of the nuts, the granulated sugar, brown sugar, butter, cocoa, flour, 1 of the eggs, the rum (if using), vanilla, and kosher

SERVES 6 TO 8

- 1⅔ cups (190 g) pecan or walnut halves (or a mix)
- ¾ cup (150 g) granulated sugar, plus more for sprinkling
- ¼ cup (55 g) packed light brown sugar
- 3 tablespoons (45 g) unsalted butter, at room temperature
- 3 tablespoons (15 g) natural or Dutch-process cocoa powder
- 1 tablespoon all-purpose flour
- 2 large eggs
- 1 tablespoon dark rum, medium amaro, or Fernet (optional)
- 1 teaspoon vanilla extract (or use 1 tablespoon if skipping liquor)
- 1 teaspoon Diamond Crystal or ½ teaspoon Morton kosher salt
- 1 standard disk A Good Crust (page 27)
- ¼ cup (45 g) roughly chopped bittersweet chocolate
- Flaky sea salt

salt and pulse until mostly smooth. If not baking the galette immediately, refrigerate the frangipane in an airtight container for up to 1 week; bring to room temperature by letting it sit out until spreadable (for up to 2 hours) before using.

4 Preheat the oven to 425°F (220°C) with a rack positioned in the center. Line a sheet pan with parchment paper.

5 Roll the dough into a round or rectangle and set it on the lined sheet pan using the Basic Method (page 34).

6 Spoon the frangipane into the crust, leaving a 3-inch (7.5 cm) border. Scatter the remaining nuts and the chopped chocolate over the surface. Fold the edges of the crust over the filling toward the center, overlapping and pleating as desired. Freeze the galette on the sheet pan for 10 minutes.

7 In a small bowl, beat the remaining egg to make an egg wash. Remove the galette from the freezer and brush the exposed crust with the egg wash. Sprinkle more granulated sugar over the crust.

8 Bake until the crust is starting to turn golden, 12 to 15 minutes (if using a cocoa crust variation, look for the crust to darken slightly). Reduce the oven temperature to 375°F (190°C) and continue to bake until the filling is puffed and the crust is deeply golden brown, another 20 to 30 minutes, rotating the sheet pan front to back halfway through. If the nuts get very dark before 20 minutes (check at the halfway point), tent the filling with foil and continue baking.

9 Remove the galette from the oven and sprinkle with some flaky sea salt. Cool, uncovered, for 30 minutes or up to 8 hours.

10 Slice and serve.

Leftovers can be stored in an airtight container in the refrigerator or at room temperature for up to 3 days. Reheat if desired (but it's pretty great cold) on a sheet pan in a 350°F (180°C) oven until warmed through, about 10 minutes.

CRUST VARIATION OPTIONS: Cocoa (page 39), Buckwheat (page 39)

SERVE WITH: A cup of Earl Grey tea, especially on winter afternoons

RIGHT-SIDE-UP PINEAPPLE

SERVES 6 TO 8

4- to 5-pound (1.8 to 2.3 kg) pineapple (see Notes), washed, stem removed

½ cup (100 g) sugar, plus more for sprinkling

2 tablespoons grated lime zest

1 teaspoon Diamond Crystal or ½ teaspoon Morton kosher salt

2 tablespoons dark rum, pineapple juice, or water

1 tablespoon cornstarch

2 tablespoons fresh lime juice

1 standard disk A Good Crust (page 27)

11 Maraschino cherries, stemmed

Egg wash: 1 large egg, beaten

Flaky sea salt

CRUST VARIATION OPTION: Cocoa (page 39)

SERVE WITH: Unsweetened whipped cream

You've heard of pineapple upside-down cake—meet right-side-up pineapple galette. It starts with a layer of quick pineapple jam, enhanced with dark rum and lime. (Make a double batch if you'd like; this stuff is excellent spread over buttered toast or between layers of vanilla cake.) Lay pineapple rings over the jam, then dot the negative space with Maraschino cherries.

NOTES: *If you can't find (or prefer not to deal with) a whole fresh pineapple, use cubed fresh pineapple for the filling (roughly chop it before starting the jam) and juice-packed canned pineapple rings for the top. The latter will be cored, but be sure to dry them well on kitchen towels or paper towels before baking.*

If your pineapple is underripe, it will be slightly dry and firm. As you cook the chopped pineapple, add up to ¼ cup (60 g) water or pineapple juice to encourage it to break down.

1 Halve the pineapple crosswise. Placing each half cut-side down, use a knife to slice off the rind. Slice half of the pineapple off the core and roughly chop it until you have about 3 cups (570 g). Reserve the remaining pineapple half.

2 In a medium saucepan, combine the sugar and lime zest and rub with your fingers until the sugar is slightly moistened and fragrant. Stir in the chopped pineapple and kosher salt. Cook the mixture over medium heat, stirring occasionally, until the juices come to a simmer. Continue to cook, using a wooden spoon to smash the pineapple and encourage it to break down, until the mixture looks like a chunky, loose jam, 10 to 15 minutes.

Recipe continues

3 Meanwhil, set up a large bowl of ice and water for an ice bath.

4 In a small bowl, stir together the rum and cornstarch until it forms a smooth slurry. Stir the cornstarch slurry into the pineapple mixture and continue to cook, stirring often and reducing the heat to ensure the mixture doesn't scorch (it's okay if it caramelizes a bit), until the mixture gets thicker, another 8 to 10 minutes. You should be able to drag a spatula through the mixture and cleanly see the bottom of the pot as the filling slowly oozes over.

5 Remove from the heat, scrape into a medium bowl, and set in the ice bath. Let cool to room temperature, about 20 minutes. Stir in the lime juice and set aside (or refrigerate in an airtight container for up to 1 week).

6 When you're ready to bake, slice 6 rounds about ¼ inch (6 mm) thick from the remaining pineapple half. Use a paring knife to cut a circle in the center, removing the center core from each round. If needed, trim each slice to be no larger than 4 inches (10 cm) wide. Snack on or save any excess pineapple for another use.

7 Preheat the oven to 425°F (220°C) with a rack positioned in the center. Line a sheet pan with parchment paper.

8 Roll the dough into a round and set it on the lined sheet pan using the Basic Method (page 34).

9 Spoon the jam into the crust, leaving a 2-inch (5 cm) border. Arrange the pineapple rings over the jam (try to get at least 3 in the center, then trim the others as needed to fit). Place a cherry into the center of each pineapple ring, and dot the rest over exposed areas of jam. Fold the edges of the crust over the filling toward the center, overlapping and pleating as desired. Freeze the galette on the sheet pan for 10 minutes.

10 Remove the galette from the freezer and brush the egg wash over the exposed crust. Sprinkle more sugar over the entire galette.

11 Bake until the crust is starting to turn golden, 12 to 15 minutes. Reduce the oven temperature to 375°F (190°C) and continue to bake until the jam is bubbling and the crust is deeply golden brown, another 40 to 50 minutes, rotating the sheet pan front to back halfway through.

12 Remove the galette from the oven and sprinkle with some flaky sea salt. Cool, uncovered, for 30 minutes or up to 2 hours.

13 Slice and serve.

Leftovers can be stored at room temperature, loosely covered, for up to 2 days. Reheat on a sheet pan in a 350°F (180°C) oven until warmed through, about 10 minutes.

ON MARASCHINO CHERRIES

Dark Luxardo-brand marasca cherries swimming in thick Maraschino syrup have the most superior flavor and texture in the preserved cherry realm— save the rest of the jar for cocktails and sundaes. But nostalgia for the classic cake might point you in the direction of fluorescent fire engine–red Maraschino cherries, which are bottled under numerous brand names and widely accessible, not to mention far cheaper. Either will do the job well.

THE ANYTHING GOES GALETTE

With a disk of A Good Crust in hand and access to produce, you don't *really* need a recipe for a simple sweet or savory galette. Here's a method you can turn to in a pinch.

Roll out **1 standard disk of A Good Crust** (page 27) into a round or rectangle using the **Basic Method** (page 34). Refrigerate on a parchment-lined sheet pan while you make the filling.

FOR A SWEET GALETTE: Toss together **1¼ pounds (565 g) fruit** (chopped or sliced into ½-inch/13 mm pieces), **⅓ cup (65 g) sugar, 2 tablespoons cornstarch** (3 tablespoons/25 g if using berries), **1 tablespoon fresh lemon juice or apple cider vinegar,** and **a couple of big pinches of kosher salt**. Spoon the filling into the crust, leaving a 2-inch (5 cm) border. Fold the edges of the crust over the filling, pleating as you'd like. Freeze the galette for 10 minutes. Beat **1 large egg** to blend, brush it over the edges of the crust, sprinkling with more **sugar** if you'd like. Bake at 425°F (220°C) for 12 to 15 minutes, until the crust is lightly golden. Reduce the oven temperature to 375°F (190°C) and continue to bake until the crust is deeply golden brown, another 40 to 50 minutes, rotating the pan front to back halfway through.

FOR A SAVORY GALETTE: Toss together **1¼ pounds (565 g) precooked or raw vegetables** (chopped or sliced into ½-inch/13 mm pieces; if using, salt raw tomatoes, eggplant, or summer squash and dry on a towel for 10 minutes), **½ cup (50 g) grated or shredded cheese** (such as Parmesan, Cheddar, or Gruyère), **2 tablespoons olive oil, 1 tablespoon fresh lemon juice or apple cider vinegar,** and **a couple of big pinches of kosher salt**. Spoon the filling into the crust, leaving a 2-inch (5 cm) border. Fold the edges of the crust over the filling, pleating as you'd like. Freeze the galette for 10 minutes. Beat **1 large egg** to blend, brush it over the edges of the crust, then sprinkle with **freshly ground black pepper** if you'd like. Bake at 425°F (220°C) for 12 to 15 minutes, until the crust is lightly golden. Reduce the oven temperature to 375°F (190°C) and continue to bake until the crust is deeply golden brown, another 40 to 50 minutes, rotating the pan front to back halfway through.

WINTER SQUASH AND ROOTS

Shredded Carrot with All the Herbs
138

Crumble-Topped Kabocha Squash
140

Beet, Cherry, and Radicchio
145

Buttered, Salted Radish
147

Mixed Sweet Potato and Harissa
150

Roasted and Raw Fennel
153

The winter blues are called SAD for a reason. While seasonal affective disorder technically shows up as a result of less sunlight, fatigue and hopelessness can also manifest at the grocery store, where the only produce in sight consists of chunky root vegetables. But what if you embrace those ingredients and beat that seasonal funk at its own game? This chapter celebrates produce that's around through the cold months, including winter squash, beets, sweet potatoes, and carrots, manipulating the ingredients to show off their strengths.

Embrace bold condiments and seasonings in these galettes, like harissa paste, nutritional yeast, za'atar, preserved lemon, and ras el hanout. Layer in other flavorful produce available any time of year (fennel, radicchio, even frozen cherries). Most of all, rethink the best ways to highlight those stars of the show—squash mustn't always be savory, carrots can be caramelized like onion, and radishes are excellent roasted with butter.

SHREDDED CARROT WITH ALL THE HERBS

- 1¼ pounds (565 g) carrots (about 7 medium), scrubbed and trimmed (no need to peel)
- 6 garlic cloves
- ¼ cup (50 g) plus 1 tablespoon olive oil
- 1 tablespoon za'atar or ras el hanout (see Notes)
- 1½ teaspoons Diamond Crystal or ¾ teaspoon Morton kosher salt, plus more to taste
- ½ teaspoon red pepper flakes
- ½ preserved lemon (30 g), very finely chopped, seeds removed; or 2 tablespoons preserved lemon paste (see Notes)
- 1 standard disk A Good Crust (page 27)
- Egg wash: 1 large egg, beaten
- 2 large shallots (4½ ounces/ 125 g) or 1 small red onion, thinly sliced
- 2 tablespoons red or white wine vinegar
- Freshly ground black pepper
- 1 cup (20 g) mixed fresh herb leaves, such as parsley, cilantro, mint, and/or dill, roughly chopped

For those who detest soft cooked carrots but don't feel like mimicking a horse as they munch the vegetable raw, I have a suggestion: grated, lightly caramelized carrots, which release some moisture as they're cooked. You avoid a soggy-bottomed pastry, but the veg hangs on to some texture as it bakes, becoming fork-tender, not mushy. Temper the sweet carrots with plenty of spices and preserved lemon. After baking, vinegar-marinated shallot and a pile of herbs over the top keep it vibrant.

NOTES: *Woodsy-floral za'atar brings excitement to spring baking; earthy ras el hanout is rooted in warm spices, which is ideal for cozy winter meals.*

Whole lemons, preserved or fresh, are edible. Since the seeds are bitter, I remove them, but otherwise use the entire lemon (peel, pith, and flesh). If you can't find preserved lemons or preserved lemon paste, swap in ½ small lemon and ½ teaspoon Diamond Crystal or ¼ teaspoon Morton kosher salt.

1 Use the large holes of a box grater or the large shredding disk on a food processor to grate the carrots and garlic.

2 Heat ¼ cup (50 g) of the oil in a Dutch oven or large deep skillet over medium heat. Stir in the shredded carrots and garlic, za'atar, salt, and pepper flakes. (It may look like too many carrots, but they'll cook down.) Cook, stirring occasionally, until the mixture is slightly soft and lightly caramelized, 15 to 25 minutes. If the mixture starts to singe, reduce the heat to medium-low.

3 Meanwhile, set up a large bowl of ice and water for an ice bath.

4 Remove the carrots from the heat, scrape into a medium bowl, and set in the ice bath. Let cool to room temperature, about 30 minutes.

5 Stir the preserved lemon into the carrot mixture. If not baking the galette immediately, transfer the mixture to an airtight container and refrigerate for up to 2 days.

6 Preheat the oven to 425°F (220°C) with a rack positioned in the center. Line a sheet pan with parchment paper.

7 Roll the dough into a rectangle and set it on the lined sheet pan using the Basic Method (page 34).

8 Spoon the carrot mixture into the crust, leaving a 1½-inch (4 cm) border. Fold the edges of the crust over the filling toward the center, overlapping and pleating as desired. Freeze the galette on the sheet pan for 10 minutes.

9 Remove the galette from the freezer and brush the egg wash over the exposed crust. Drizzle the remaining 1 tablespoon oil over the filling.

10 Bake until the crust is starting to turn golden, 12 to 15 minutes. Reduce the oven temperature to 375°F (190°C) and continue to bake until the filling is starting to brown and the crust is deeply golden brown, another 35 to 40 minutes, rotating the sheet pan front to back halfway through.

11 Remove the galette from the oven and cool, uncovered, for 15 minutes or up to 8 hours.

12 While the galette bakes, in a small bowl, toss together the shallots, vinegar, and salt and black pepper to taste.

13 Before serving, scatter the shallot mixture and herbs over the galette. Slice and serve.

Leftovers can be stored in an airtight container in the refrigerator for up to 24 hours; if you don't mind wilting the topping, reheat on a sheet pan in a 350°F (180°C) oven until warmed through, about 10 minutes.

CRUST VARIATION OPTIONS: Whole Wheat (page 39), Buckwheat (page 39)

SERVE WITH: Garlicky Yogurt (page 43)

CRUMBLE-TOPPED KABOCHA SQUASH

SERVES 6 TO 8

3 tablespoons (40 g) light brown sugar

2 tablespoons unrefined coconut oil or unsalted butter, melted and cooled

1 tablespoon apple cider vinegar

½ teaspoon Diamond Crystal or ¼ teaspoon Morton kosher salt

1¼ pounds (565 g) kabocha (about ½ medium) or acorn squash (about 1 medium), seeds removed, no need to peel (see opposite)

1 standard disk A Good Crust (page 27)

2 batches Crumble Topping (page 41)

Egg wash: 1 large egg, beaten

Demerara or granulated sugar

Flaky sea salt

CRUST VARIATION OPTIONS: Whole Wheat (page 39), Cocoa (page 39)

SERVE WITH: Vanilla ice cream or Maple Whip (page 42), your favorite amaro

Every time I eat roasted kabocha squash, which bakes up almost fudgy in texture, I think: *I need to use this in a dessert*. I'm making good on that promise. To highlight its sweetness, sandwich the squash between clumps of spiced oat crumble. The crumble will caramelize underneath the squash and partially melt into delicate freckles across the galette's surface. Those who are bored by pumpkin pie may find this to be their new favorite fall sweet.

1 Preheat the oven to 425°F (220°C) with a rack positioned in the center. Line a sheet pan with parchment paper.

2 In a large bowl, stir together the brown sugar, coconut oil, vinegar, and kosher salt.

3 Slice the squash into 1-inch (2.5 cm) wedges or ½-inch (13 mm) chunks and toss with the sugar mixture.

4 Roll the dough into a round or rectangle and set it on the lined sheet pan using the Basic Method (page 34).

5 Sprinkle about half of the crumble topping over the crust in an even layer, leaving a 2-inch (5 cm) border. Leaving any excess liquid in the bowl, arrange the squash over the crumble in a single layer. Sprinkle over the remaining crumble topping in bite-size chunks. Fold the edges of the crust over the filling toward the center, overlapping and pleating as desired. Freeze the galette on the sheet pan for 10 minutes.

6 Remove the galette from the freezer and brush the egg wash over the exposed crust. Sprinkle the crust with demerara sugar.

7 Bake until the crust is starting to turn golden, 12 to 15 minutes. Reduce the oven temperature to 375°F (190°C) and continue to bake until the squash is tender (a paring knife or cake tester should easily slide in) and the crust is deeply golden brown, another 45 to 55 minutes, rotating the sheet pan front to back halfway through.

8 Remove the galette from the oven and sprinkle with some flaky sea salt. Cool, uncovered, for 30 minutes or up to 8 hours. Slice and serve.

Leftovers can be stored at room temperature, loosely covered, for up to 2 days. Reheat on a sheet pan in a 350°F (180°C) oven until warmed through, about 10 minutes.

TIPS FOR CUTTING A BIG SQUASH

If you're nervous about slicing a large kabocha squash, try microwaving it (whole) for 1 minute. This will slightly soften the skin and flesh, making it easier for your knife to pierce through.

Arranging sliced squash wedges in a spiral pattern makes a stunning presentation, but cutting the large bulbous produce can be (literally) tough. Use a large, sharp chef's knife to halve a rinsed and dried squash through the root end—no need to peel—then scoop out and discard the seeds and pulp. Remove the stem, then place one squash half cut-side down. From there, slice through the skin into wedges, or cut into chunks. (Alternatively, buy cubed butternut squash at the supermarket— it's likely the only variety available where the knifework is done for you, and the flavor and texture are only slightly different from kabocha.)

BEET, CHERRY, AND RADICCHIO

A good galette should be flavor-driven. But oftentimes color plays a role. Here shades of red in the form of beets, cherries, and onion create the foundation of a savory galette. Creamy feta bakes alongside the produce but doesn't melt like other cheeses, offering pockets of salty tang to offset the sweet. Cover the baked galette with a blanket of more red: radicchio leaves, dressed in oil and vinegar.

NOTE: *If you can't find precooked beets, scrub 12 ounces (340 g) beets (2 to 3 medium). Preheat the oven to 425°F (220°C) with a rack positioned in the center. Place each beet on a small piece of foil and drizzle each with 1 tablespoon olive oil. Wrap the beets in the foil and roast until tender, 40 to 60 minutes depending on their size. Let the beets cool to touch, then use paper towels to rub off the skins. Let cool completely, about 1 hour. Beets can be stored in an airtight container in the refrigerator for up to 3 days.*

1 In a large bowl, combine the beets, cherries, feta, onion, vinegar, 1 tablespoon of the olive oil, the coriander, kosher salt, and lots of pepper.

2 Preheat the oven to 425°F (220°C) with a rack positioned in the center. Line a sheet pan with parchment paper.

3 Roll the dough into a round and set it on the lined sheet pan using the Basic Method (page 34).

Recipe continues

SERVES 4 TO 6

12 ounces (340 g) peeled cooked beets (2 to 3 medium; see Note), cut into ½-inch (13 mm) chunks

1 cup (155 g) pitted sweet or tart cherries (fresh or frozen), halved

1 cup (155 g) crumbled feta cheese or ¼-inch (6 mm) cubes Halloumi

1 small red onion (4½ ounces/ 125 g) or 2 large shallots, thinly sliced (about ½ cup)

2 tablespoons distilled white or red wine vinegar, plus more for serving

2 tablespoons olive oil

2 teaspoons ground coriander

½ teaspoon Diamond Crystal or ¼ teaspoon Morton kosher salt

Freshly ground black pepper

1 standard disk A Good Crust (page 27)

Egg wash: 1 large egg, beaten

Flaky sea salt

½ small head radicchio, leaves separated, for serving

Good extra-virgin olive oil, for serving

4 Leaving any excess liquid in the bowl, spoon the beet mixture into the crust, leaving a 2-inch (5 cm) border. Fold the edges of the crust over the filling toward the center, overlapping and pleating as desired. Freeze the galette on the sheet pan for 10 minutes.

5 Remove the galette from the freezer and brush the egg wash over the exposed crust. Sprinkle the edges with more pepper. Drizzle the remaining 1 tablespoon olive oil over the filling.

6 Bake until the crust is starting to turn golden, 12 to 15 minutes. Reduce the oven temperature to 375°F (190°C) and continue to bake until the filling is starting to brown and the crust is deeply golden brown, another 40 to 50 minutes, rotating the sheet pan front to back halfway through.

7 Remove the galette from the oven and sprinkle with some flaky sea salt. Cool, uncovered, for 30 minutes or up to 2 hours.

8 Before serving, arrange the radicchio over the top of the galette. Drizzle with extra-virgin olive oil and more vinegar. Slice and serve.

Leftovers can be stored in an airtight container in the refrigerator for up to 24 hours; if you don't mind wilting the radicchio, reheat on a sheet pan in a 350°F (180°C) oven until warmed through, about 10 minutes.

BUTTERED, SALTED RADISH

The first time I tried radishes with butter and salt, my life changed. Rich, fatty butter mellows the peppery root, and craggy pieces of flaky salt offer crunch and of course proper seasoning. In my eyes, there is no better bite. (Except, sometimes, when you swap the butter for a thick wedge of cheese.) This galette transforms the snack into a full dish. Round red supermarket radishes will do here, but there's something extra-special about the uneven shape and ripples of pink, purple, and green running through heirloom varieties available at the farmers market and some specialty grocers. Salty cheese and brined white anchovy offer a foil to the peppery radishes via funk and salt.

NOTE: *Use a mandoline if you have one to get even, thin slices of radishes and onion.*

1 In a large bowl, toss together the radishes, onion, lemon juice, and kosher salt. Let sit for at least 10 minutes and up to 30 minutes.

2 Preheat the oven to 425°F (220°C) with a rack positioned in the center. Line a sheet pan with parchment paper.

3 Roll the dough into a round or rectangle and set it on the lined sheet pan using the Basic Method (page 34).

Recipe continues

SERVES 4 TO 6

1 pound (455 g) mixed radishes, greens removed, thinly sliced into rounds (see Note)

1 small red onion (4½ ounces/ 125 g) or 2 large shallots, thinly sliced into rounds (about ½ cup)

2 tablespoons fresh lemon juice or distilled white vinegar

1 teaspoon Diamond Crystal or ½ teaspoon Morton kosher salt

1 standard disk A Good Crust (page 27)

½ cup (70 g) shredded Comté, Piave, or Parmesan cheese

Egg wash: 1 large egg, beaten

Flaky sea salt, for sprinkling

2 tablespoons unsalted butter, cut into small pieces

Brined white or oil-packed anchovies, for serving (optional, but not really)

CRUST VARIATION OPTION: Whole Wheat (page 39)

SERVE WITH: Roast chicken and a bottle of very cold light red wine

4 Scatter the cheese over the crust, leaving a 2-inch (5 cm) border. Leaving any excess liquid in the bowl, arrange the radish mixture over the cheese. Fold the edges of the crust over the filling toward the center, overlapping and pleating as desired. Freeze the galette on the sheet pan for 10 minutes.

5 Remove the galette from the freezer and brush the egg wash over the exposed crust. Sprinkle the crust with a pinch of flaky sea salt. Scatter the butter over the exposed filling, focusing on the center.

6 Bake until the crust is starting to turn golden, 12 to 15 minutes. Reduce the oven temperature to 375°F (190°C) and continue to bake until the radishes are just starting to wrinkle and the crust is deeply golden brown, another 40 to 50 minutes, rotating the sheet pan front to back halfway through.

7 Remove the galette from the oven and cool, uncovered, for 15 minutes or up to 2 hours.

8 Top with anchovies (if using), slice, and serve.

Best eaten day-of.

MIXED SWEET POTATO AND HARISSA

SERVES 8 TO 10

⅓ cup (70 g) harissa (see Notes), any heat level

3 tablespoons (40 g) olive oil, plus more as needed

2 tablespoons nutritional yeast

½ preserved lemon (30 g), very finely chopped, seeds removed; or 2 tablespoons preserved lemon paste

4 garlic cloves, grated

1 tablespoon cumin seeds

2 teaspoons ground coriander

2 teaspoons Diamond Crystal or 1 teaspoon Morton kosher salt

2¼ pounds (1 kg) medium or small mixed sweet potatoes, scrubbed and very thinly sliced into rounds (see Notes)

Cooking spray or vegetable oil, for the pan

1 XL disk A Good Crust (page 27)

Egg wash: 1 large egg, beaten

Pomegranate molasses (optional), for serving

A centerpiece pastry if there ever was one, this extra-tall specimen is ready to compete with any roast on the holiday table. For a range of flavor, texture, and color, embrace multiple varieties of sweet potato, or even layer in seeded, thinly sliced winter squash like delicata, butternut, acorn, or kabocha (no need to peel). To cut through the sweetness of the filling, toss the potatoes with salty preserved lemon and nutritional yeast, plus a good dollop of warming harissa.

NOTES: *Seek out harissa sold in jars or large containers; it will have a looser consistency than versions sold in a tube.*

Look for sweet potatoes that are between 3 and 5 inches (7.5 and 13 cm) long and not more than 2 inches (5 cm) wide. If you can only find larger sweet potatoes, it will be easier to halve them lengthwise and then slice them into half-moons instead of rounds.

1 Preheat the oven to 425°F (220°C) with a rack positioned in the center. Place a sheet pan in the oven to preheat.

2 In a large bowl, whisk together the harissa, olive oil, nutritional yeast, preserved lemon, garlic, cumin seeds, coriander, and salt. This should be roughly the consistency of marinara sauce; if it's thick like tomato paste (some harissas are thicker than others), thin with another 1 to 2 tablespoons of oil. Add the sweet potatoes and toss to coat.

Recipe continues

SPECIAL EQUIPMENT:
9- or 10-inch (23 or 25 cm)
springform pan

**CRUST VARIATION
OPTIONS:** Whole Wheat
(page 39), Buckwheat (page 39)

SERVE WITH: Garlicky
Yogurt (page 43) or Zingy Tahini
(page 43), Thanksgiving dinner

3 Grease a 9- or 10-inch (23 or 25 cm) springform pan with cooking spray. Roll the dough into a round and fit it into the pan using the Pan Method (page 36).

4 Spoon the filling into the crust. Use kitchen scissors to trim the edges of the dough so it can fold over the filling by about 2 inches (5 cm) or less. (Save the trimmings for Crispy, Flaky "Shortbread," page 45.) Fold the edges of the crust over the filling toward the center, overlapping and pleating as desired. Freeze the galette for 10 minutes.

5 Remove the galette from the freezer and brush the egg wash over the exposed crust.

6 Place the springform pan on the preheated sheet pan in the oven. Bake until the crust is starting to turn golden, 12 to 15 minutes. Reduce the oven temperature to 375°F (190°C) and continue to bake until the potatoes are tender and the crust is deeply golden brown and starting to pull away from the edges of the pan, another 75 to 85 minutes, rotating the pan front to back halfway through. If the exposed filling starts to singe in places before 75 minutes, tent with foil and continue baking.

7 Remove the galette from the oven and cool, uncovered, for 1 hour or up to 8 hours before unmolding. Slice and serve, drizzled with pomegranate molasses (if using).

Leftovers can be stored at room temperature, loosely covered, for up to 24 hours or in the refrigerator for up to 3 days. Reheat on a sheet pan in a 350°F (180°C) oven until warmed through, about 10 minutes.

ROASTED AND RAW FENNEL

These tiny, elegant galettes are an homage to one of my favorite restaurant salads, the finocchio at Altro Paradiso in Manhattan. If you've had the dish, you know how good it is for such a minimal ingredient list; if not, you're about to find out, so either way, lucky you. Reimagined as a galette, it offers the best of both fennel-worlds. Because the only thing better than raw fennel (crunchy, very anisey) is roasted fennel (sweet like caramelized onion, soft, less anisey). The fennel mingles with mellow Castelvetrano olives, salty cheese, and lots of lemon, most of which is baked in the galettes and the rest of which is set aside to pile atop each before devouring.

NOTE: *The recipe makes 4 small galettes but is easily doubled if you're serving a larger group. Bake on two sheet pans on racks positioned in the upper and lower thirds of the oven, and switch racks halfway through baking.*

1 Preheat the oven to 375°F (190°C) with a rack positioned in the center. Line a sheet pan with parchment paper.

2 In a large bowl, combine the sliced fennel, olives, lemon zest, lemon juice, olive oil, salt, and a few grinds of pepper.

3 Roll out 4 dough rounds using the Tiny Method (page 36) and arrange evenly spaced on the lined sheet pan.

Recipe continues

MAKES 4 SMALL GALETTES

- 1 pound (455 g) fennel bulbs (about 2 medium), bulbs and stalks very thinly sliced, any fronds reserved
- ¾ cup (115 g) chopped pitted Castelvetrano olives
- 2 tablespoons grated lemon zest
- ¼ cup (55 g) fresh lemon juice, plus more to taste
- 2 tablespoons olive oil
- ½ teaspoon Diamond Crystal or ¼ teaspoon Morton kosher salt, plus more to taste
- Freshly ground black pepper
- 1 standard disk A Good Crust (page 27)
- 1 cup (100 g) shredded pecorino or Parmesan cheese
- Egg wash: 1 large egg, beaten
- Good extra-virgin olive oil, for serving
- Chopped toasted hazelnuts or almonds (optional)

CRUST VARIATION OPTION: Whole Wheat (page 39)

4 Sprinkle 1 tablespoon of pecorino in the center of a dough round, leaving a 2-inch (5 cm) border. Leaving any excess liquid in the bowl, arrange ½ cup (55 g) of the fennel mixture over the cheese. Brush the border around the filling with some egg wash. Fold the edges of the crust over the filling toward the center, overlapping and pleating as desired. Repeat with the remaining 3 dough rounds.

5 Freeze the galettes on the sheet pan for 15 minutes. Refrigerate the remaining fennel mixture.

6 Remove the galettes from the freezer and brush more egg wash over the exposed crusts.

7 Bake until the crusts are deeply golden brown, 35 to 45 minutes, rotating the sheet pan front to back halfway through. If any of the edges unfold during the first half of baking, you can use a butter knife to gently refold them when rotating the pan.

8 Remove the galettes from the oven and cool, uncovered, for 15 minutes while you finish the topping.

9 To the bowl with the remaining fennel mixture, add the remaining shredded cheese and reserved fennel fronds and toss. Season with more salt, pepper, and lemon juice to taste. Divide the raw fennel mixture in lofty piles over the galettes, then drizzle with extra-virgin olive oil and sprinkle over the hazelnuts (if using) before serving.

Once topped, the galettes are best eaten within 2 hours. Without topping, leftovers can be stored in an airtight container in the refrigerator for up to 2 days. Reheat on a sheet pan in a 350°F (180°C) oven until warmed through, about 10 minutes.

NIGHT-SHADES AND SUMMER SQUASH

Tomatoes, eggplants, peppers, and white potatoes have something in common: They're nightshades. It may seem odd for such a wide variety of strong flavors, textures, and colors to be related, but I don't make the rules. While some nightshades are a delight to eat raw, others need a bit of zhuzhing. (Cooking with plenty of salt and oil does the trick.) While their season—and therefore when they have the best flavor—is technically summer through early fall, you're bound to find perfectly good nightshades in the supermarket year-round.

Summer squash, from standard green and yellow zucchini to flying saucer–shaped pattypan and color-blocked Zephyr squash, also tend to be misunderstood. But when they're roasted until tender over crisp, buttery pastry, you'll wonder why you ever passed on them. Like nightshades, summer squash can be found most months of the year. But as their name would suggest, come summertime, these gourds are plentiful to say the least.

WARM-WEATHER TIAN

SERVES 4 TO 6

1 standard disk A Good Crust (page 27)

6 ounces (170 g) plum, Campari, or small heirloom tomatoes (2 to 3), sliced ⅛ inch (3 mm) thick

6 ounces (170 g) green and/ or yellow zucchini (2 to 3 small), sliced ⅛ inch (3 mm) thick

One 6-ounce (170 g) Japanese or Chinese eggplant, sliced ⅛ inch (3 mm) thick

3 tablespoons (40 g) olive oil

¾ teaspoon Diamond Crystal or ¼ teaspoon Morton kosher salt, plus more to taste

2 tablespoons Dijon or whole-grain mustard

6 garlic cloves, thinly sliced

1 tablespoon fresh thyme or oregano leaves, plus more for serving

Freshly ground black pepper

Egg wash: 1 large egg, beaten

CRUST VARIATION
OPTION: Whole Wheat (page 39)

SERVE WITH: Garlicky Yogurt (page 43), your favorite charcuterie, soft cheese

You've probably heard of ratatouille, the rustic Provençal dish of stewed tomatoes, eggplant, and zucchini; but how about tian? Similar to ratatouille in ingredients but far more elegant in presentation, tians feature a captivating spiral or neat rows of tiled vegetable rounds. (Fun fact: The French word *tian* refers to both the dish and the earthenware vessel in which it's traditionally baked—I think it's still okay to call it as such when baked in pastry dough.)

1 Line a sheet pan with parchment paper. Roll the dough into a round and set it on the lined sheet pan using the Basic Method (page 34). Refrigerate on the sheet pan while you make the filling (it takes a while to fill the crust so it's best for the dough to be extra-cold).

2 In a medium bowl, toss the tomatoes, zucchini, and eggplant with 2 tablespoons of the oil and the salt. Let sit for at least 10 minutes and up to 30 minutes to draw out some moisture.

3 Preheat the oven to 425°F (220°C) with a rack positioned in the center.

4 Brush the mustard over the crust, leaving a 2-inch (5 cm) border. Scatter the garlic and thyme over and season with more salt and pepper. Leaving any excess liquid in the bowl, arrange the produce in rows or concentric circles, alternating between tomatoes, zucchini, and eggplant.

5 Twist and crimp the crust border over itself to make a 1-inch (2.5 cm) border. (Alternatively, as for any other galette, fold the edges of the crust over the filling toward the center, overlapping and pleating as desired.) Freeze the galette for 10 minutes.

6 Remove the galette from the freezer and brush the egg wash over the exposed crust. Drizzle the remaining 1 tablespoon oil over the filling and season with more pepper.

7 Bake until the crust is starting to turn golden, 12 to 15 minutes. Reduce the oven temperature to 375°F (190°C) and continue to bake until the filling is starting to brown and the crust is deeply golden brown, another 40 to 50 minutes, rotating the sheet pan front to back halfway through.

8 Remove the galette from the oven and cool, uncovered, for 15 minutes or up to 8 hours.

Leftovers can be stored in an airtight container in the refrigerator for up to 3 days. Reheat on a sheet pan in a 350°F (180°C) oven until warmed through, about 10 minutes.

FOR THE PRETTIEST GALETTE

To make this galette look as uniform as possible, seek out produce that are all roughly the same circumference—about 2 inches (5 cm). In this case, straight green or yellow zucchini, slender Japanese or Chinese eggplant, and oblong plum tomatoes will tend to mimic each other's shapes most closely, but keep in mind that the galette will taste just as good even if the produce doesn't perfectly match.

POTATO, CHIPS, AND RED ONION

SERVES 4 TO 6

1 pound (480 g) russet potatoes (1 to 2), scrubbed

3 small red onions (12 ounces/ 340 g total), peeled

1½ teaspoons Diamond Crystal or ¾ teaspoon Morton kosher salt

3 tablespoons (40 g) olive oil

2 tablespoons hot or sweet smoked paprika

2 large eggs

1½ cups (65 g) salted potato chips, preferably kettle-cooked

1 standard disk A Good Crust (page 27)

Flaky sea salt

Sherry vinegar or red wine vinegar, for serving

CRUST VARIATION OPTION: Peppery (page 40)

SERVE WITH: Smoked or tinned fish, sour cream

Somewhere on the evolutionary journey a potato takes from patatas bravas to a latke is this galette. Coat shredded russets and onions in smoked paprika, finish with a glug of sherry vinegar. How *do* those potatoes get so crisp? The secret lies in a few big handfuls of potato chips baked along with the raw vegetables, mimicking the flavor while adding tons of satisfying crunch. Word to the wise: Don't skimp on the potato-squeezing step. Grab your friends and say you want to find out who's the strongest—you won't have to do any work.

1 Use the large holes of a box grater or the large shredding disk on a food processor to grate the potatoes and 2 of the onions.

2 Transfer the grated potatoes and onions to a kitchen towel and place over a large bowl. Toss the mixture with ½ teaspoon Diamond Crystal or ¼ teaspoon Morton kosher salt and let sit for 10 minutes. Gather the edges of the towel and squeeze out as much liquid as you possibly can into the bowl. Place the towel (with the potato mixture still inside) on a cutting board or plate and let the mixture sit for 5 minutes. Squeeze out the liquid into the bowl again. Keep the potato mixture in the towel. Let the liquid sit in the bowl for 5 minutes, then gently pour out the water, leaving any milky-white potato starch accumulated in the bottom of the bowl. While you're waiting, slice the remaining onion thickly into rings.

Recipe continues

3 Place the grated potato mixture in the bowl with the starch and add the remaining 1 teaspoon Diamond Crystal or ½ teaspoon Morton kosher salt, 2 tablespoons of the oil, the smoked paprika, and 1 of the eggs. Use your hands to mix everything together until well combined. Mix in the potato chips, letting them break a bit naturally but not pulverizing them.

4 Preheat the oven to 425°F (220°C) with a rack positioned in the center. Line a sheet pan with parchment paper.

5 Roll the dough into a round or rectangle and set it on the lined sheet pan using the Basic Method (page 34).

6 Spoon the grated potato mixture into the crust, leaving a 1-inch (2.5 cm) border. Scatter over the onion rings. Fold the edges of the crust over the filling toward the center, overlapping and pleating as desired. Freeze the galette on the sheet pan for 10 minutes.

7 In a small bowl, beat the remaining egg to make an egg wash. Remove the galette from the freezer and brush the egg wash over the exposed crust. Drizzle the remaining 1 tablespoon oil over the filling.

8 Bake until the crust is starting to turn golden, 12 to 15 minutes. Reduce the oven temperature to 375°F (190°C) and continue to bake until the filling is starting to brown and the crust is deeply golden brown, another 40 to 50 minutes, rotating the sheet pan front to back halfway through. If the onion rings start to get very dark before 40 minutes, tent the filling with foil and continue baking.

9 Remove the galette from the oven and sprinkle with some flaky sea salt. Cool, uncovered, for 30 minutes or up to 2 hours.

10 Drizzle with vinegar, slice, and serve.

Best eaten day-of. Leftovers can be stored loosely covered at room temperature for up to 24 hours. Reheat on a sheet pan in a 350°F (180°C) oven until warmed through, about 10 minutes.

SPICY EGGPLANT PARM

If eggplant Parmesan is on the menu, I will get it (pro move: order one for the table). I like versions that aren't super-cheesy, with eggplant fried crunchy-crisp or left thick so the flesh goes silky—none of that flabby or dry eggplant business. Delightfully, this dish is easily galette-ified. Like any good eggplant Parm, it takes some time, but the end result is worth the labor. If you happen to have homemade marinara, use it by all means; but I think Rao's does a stellar job in the jarred-sauce department.

NOTE: *Look for jarred, not raw, Calabrian chiles that are chopped or crushed and preserved in oil.*

1 Preheat the oven to 425°F (220°C) with racks positioned in the upper and lower thirds.

2 Arrange the eggplant in a single layer on two sheet pans and drizzle with the oil, tossing to coat. Sprinkle the eggplant on both sides with the salt and dried oregano. Roast until the eggplant is tender and starting to brown, 20 to 25 minutes, flipping the eggplant, switching racks, and rotating the sheet pans front to back halfway through.

3 Remove the eggplant from the oven and let cool completely, about 30 minutes. If not assembling the galette right away, after cooling to room temperature, refrigerate in an airtight container for up to 24 hours.

4 In a bowl, stir together the marinara, Calabrian chiles, and salt to taste. If not assembling the galette right away, refrigerate in an airtight container for up to 24 hours.

Recipe continues

SERVES 4 TO 6

2 pounds (910 g) Italian or globe eggplant, unpeeled, sliced into ½-inch (13 mm) rounds

6 tablespoons (80 g) olive oil

2 teaspoons Diamond Crystal or 1 teaspoon Morton kosher salt, plus more to taste

1 tablespoon dried oregano

2 cups (500 g) jarred marinara sauce

2 tablespoons jarred crushed Calabrian chiles (see Note), or 1 teaspoon red pepper flakes plus 1 teaspoon distilled white vinegar

Cooking spray or vegetable oil, for the pan

1 standard disk A Good Crust (page 27)

1 cup (100 g) finely grated Parmesan cheese

6 ounces (170 g) low-moisture mozzarella cheese, torn into bite-size pieces

Egg wash: 1 large egg, beaten

Fresh basil and/or oregano leaves (optional), for serving

5 When you're ready to assemble the galette, grease a 9- or 10-inch (23 or 25 cm) cast-iron skillet, pie plate, or cake pan with cooking spray.

6 Roll the dough into a round and fit it into the vessel using the Pan Method (page 36).

7 If it's not still on, preheat the oven to 425°F (220°C) with a rack positioned in the center. Place a sheet pan in the oven to preheat.

8 Sprinkle ¼ cup (25 g) of the Parmesan over the crust. Arrange half the eggplant in a single layer. Scatter half of the mozzarella over the eggplant. Sprinkle with another ¼ cup (25 g) of the Parmesan. Dollop ¼ cup (65 g) of the spicy sauce over the top. Repeat with the remaining half of the eggplant and mozzarella, and another ¼ cup (25 g) of the Parmesan. Dollop another ¼ cup (65 g) of the spicy sauce over (you will not use it all; reserve the rest for serving). Sprinkle with the remaining Parmesan. Fold the edges of the crust over the filling toward the center, overlapping and pleating as desired. Freeze the galette for 10 minutes.

9 Remove the galette from the freezer and brush the egg wash over the exposed crust.

10 Bake on the preheated sheet pan until the crust is starting to turn golden, 12 to 15 minutes. Reduce the oven temperature to 375°F (190°C) and continue to bake until the crust is deeply golden and starting to pull away from the sides of the skillet, another 50 to 60 minutes, rotating the pan front to back halfway through.

11 Remove the galette from the oven and cool, uncovered, for 30 minutes or up to 2 hours.

12 Top with fresh herbs (if using), slice, and serve with the remaining spicy sauce.

Recipe continues

SPECIAL EQUIPMENT: 9- or 10-inch (23 or 25 cm) cast-iron skillet, metal or ceramic pie plate, or cake pan

SERVE WITH: Iceberg salad, Italian sausage

Leftovers can be stored in an airtight container in the refrigerator for up to 3 days. Reheat on a sheet pan in a 350°F (180°C) oven until warmed through, about 15 minutes.

VARIATION

For another galette inspired by a beloved Italian eggplant dish, look to caponata. To the spicy sauce, stir in ½ cup (78 g) chopped Castelvetrano olives, 1 tablespoon brined capers, ¼ cup (48 g) golden raisins, 1 tablespoon white wine vinegar, and ½ teaspoon sugar. Use the Parmesan, but skip the mozzarella (neither are traditional caponata components, but who's mad about extra Parm?). Instead of mozzarella, layer in ½ medium red or yellow onion (80 g), thinly sliced, and 1 cup (100 g) chopped celery.

CARAMELIZED ZUCCHINI AND BACON

When shredded and gently sautéed in fat, zucchini gets jammy-sweet. (If you're not in the mood for a galette, try tossing this with pasta.) Lay parallel strips of bacon over the filling before baking—you'll slowly fry it first to render out fat to cook the zucchini and crisp the meat, then finish it in the oven.

NOTE: *Vegetarians can still make this—swap in a meatless bacon. Since it doesn't tend to render much fat, use 3 tablespoons (40 g) olive oil instead of bacon fat to caramelize the zucchini.*

1 Place the bacon in a single layer in a large nonstick or cast-iron skillet. Set over medium-low heat and cook, flipping often, until the bacon renders a lot of fat and is just starting to crisp but is not cooked all the way through (it'll finish in the oven), 10 to 15 minutes.

2 Transfer the bacon to a paper towel–lined plate, leaving the rendered fat in the pan. Let cool to room temperature (or up to 2 hours). If not baking the galette immediately, transfer the bacon and its fat into separate airtight containers and refrigerate for up to 2 days.

3 When you're ready to make the filling, use the large holes of a box grater or the large shredding disk on a food processor to grate the zucchini and garlic.

4 Return the bacon fat (you should have about 3 tablespoons/40 g; supplement with olive oil if needed) to the skillet and set over medium-high heat. Stir in the grated zucchini and garlic, salt, and pepper. Cook, stirring occasionally, until the zucchini

SERVES 4 TO 6

6 slices (5½ ounces/160 g) thin-cut bacon

2 pounds (910 g) zucchini or summer squash

6 garlic cloves

Olive oil, as needed

1 teaspoon Diamond Crystal or ½ teaspoon Morton kosher salt

½ teaspoon freshly ground black pepper

1 standard disk A Good Crust (page 27)

1 cup (115 g) shredded Gruyère cheese

Egg wash: 1 large egg, beaten

Really good tomatoes, sliced into wedges and salted, for serving

CRUST VARIATION OPTIONS: Whole Wheat (page 39), Buckwheat (page 39)

starts to look jammy, not watery, 20 to 30 minutes. If you find the zucchini is looking charred or fried instead of soft and sticky, reduce the heat to medium.

5 Meanwhile, set up a large bowl of ice and water for an ice bath.

6 Remove the zucchini from the heat, scrape into a medium bowl, and set in the ice bath. Let cool to room temperature, about 30 minutes. If not baking the galette immediately, after 20 minutes, transfer to an airtight container and refrigerate for up to 2 days. Let it come to room temperature before using.

7 Preheat the oven to 425°F (220°C) with a rack positioned in the center. Line a sheet pan with parchment paper.

8 Roll the dough into a rectangle and set it on the lined sheet pan using the Basic Method (page 34).

9 Stir the Gruyère into the zucchini mixture. Spoon the zucchini mixture into the crust, leaving a 1½-inch (4 cm) border. Lay the bacon strips evenly over the zucchini mixture. Fold the edges of the crust over the filling toward the center, overlapping and pleating as desired. Freeze the galette on the sheet pan for 10 minutes.

10 Remove the galette from the freezer and brush the egg wash over the exposed crust.

11 Bake until the crust is starting to turn golden, 12 to 15 minutes. Reduce the oven temperature to 375°F (190°C) and continue to bake until the bacon looks cooked through and the crust is deeply golden brown, another 30 to 35 minutes, rotating the pan front to back halfway through.

12 Remove the galette from the oven and cool, uncovered, for 15 minutes or up to 2 hours.

13 Slice and serve, with the tomatoes over the top or alongside.

Leftovers can be stored in an airtight container in the refrigerator for up to 2 days. Reheat on a sheet pan in a 350°F (180°C) oven until warmed through, about 10 minutes.

SPICE-DUSTED HEIRLOOM TOMATO

SERVES 4 TO 6

1 pound (455 g) small mixed heirloom tomatoes, sliced ¼ inch (6 mm) thick

8 ounces (225 g) mixed cherry, Sungold, or grape tomatoes, halved

1 teaspoon Diamond Crystal or ½ teaspoon Morton kosher salt, plus more to taste

1 teaspoon fennel seeds, roughly crushed

1 teaspoon cumin seeds

1 teaspoon mild chile flakes, such as Aleppo pepper or gochugaru

½ teaspoon ground coriander

2 tablespoons mayonnaise

4 garlic cloves, grated

1 standard disk A Good Crust (page 27)

Egg wash: 1 large egg, beaten

1 tablespoon olive oil

Flaky sea salt

CRUST VARIATION OPTION: Cornmeal (page 39)

Sweet, juicy heirloom tomatoes are ideal in a galette, their acidity offset by the buttery pastry. I give this one the same treatment as my tomato toast: fragrant seed- and chile flake–dusted tomatoes over a layer of garlicky mayonnaise. The bottom will turn out the crispest with smaller tomatoes, which contain more flesh and less watery pulp, but really, any size will do.

1 In a large bowl, gently toss together the tomatoes and kosher salt. Let sit for at least 10 minutes and up to 30 minutes. Set up a kitchen towel on a work surface. Leaving any excess liquid in the bowl, transfer the tomatoes to the towel (see page 174). Pat the tomatoes dry.

2 While the tomatoes are sitting, in a small bowl, stir together the fennel, cumin seeds, chile flakes, and coriander. In another small bowl, stir together the mayonnaise, garlic, and a pinch of kosher salt.

3 Preheat the oven to 425°F (220°C) with a rack positioned in the center. Line a sheet pan with parchment paper.

4 Roll the dough into a round and set it on the lined sheet pan using the Basic Method (page 34).

5 Spoon the garlicky mayonnaise into the crust, leaving a 2-inch (5 cm) border. Layer the tomatoes over the mayonnaise (start with larger ones, then tile in smaller ones in open spaces, overlapping as needed). Sprinkle the tomatoes with the spice mix. Fold the edges of the crust over the filling toward the center, overlapping and pleating as desired. Freeze the galette on the sheet pan for 10 minutes.

Recipe continues

6 Remove the galette from the freezer and brush the egg wash over the exposed crust. Drizzle the oil over the filling.

7 Bake until the crust is starting to turn golden, 12 to 15 minutes. Reduce the oven temperature to 375°F (190°C) and continue to bake until the filling is starting to brown and the crust is deeply golden brown, another 40 to 50 minutes, rotating the sheet pan front to back halfway through.

8 Remove the galette from the oven and sprinkle with some flaky sea salt. Cool, uncovered, for 20 minutes or up to 2 hours.

9 Slice and serve.

Leftovers can be stored in an airtight container in the refrigerator for up to 3 days. Reheat on a sheet pan in a 350°F (180°C) oven until warmed through, about 10 minutes.

VARIATION

Riff on the beloved summer sandwich with a BLT galette: Skip the spice mix and olive oil; after the galette bakes for 25 minutes at 375°F (190°C), remove from the oven and top the tomatoes with 3 slices of roughly chopped, uncooked thin-cut bacon. Return to the oven and continue to bake until the bacon is crisp, another 20 to 25 minutes. Let cool for 20 minutes or up to 2 hours, then top with torn leaves of tender lettuce, such as Little Gem, tossed with a little fresh lemon juice, plus a sprinkle of flaky sea salt and black pepper.

It's Not a Galette, But. . .

Don't toss that salty-sweet tomato juice! After removing the salted tomatoes from the bowl, strain the liquid through a fine-mesh sieve and use it as the base of a vinaigrette or to finish a pasta dish. It even works in a martini: I like a ratio of one part dry gin or vodka, one part dry vermouth, and one-half part tomato water, stirred or shaken with ice and garnished with an olive and/or a lemon twist.

VINEGARED PEPPERS AND BIG BEANS

A no-brainer dinner for me is something saucy and veg-filled tossed with beans, a few slices of toast alongside to mop up the mess. That served as inspiration for this late-summer galette, which lets bell peppers really show off. Any white beans will work here, but larger specimens like butter or gigante are especially fun folded in.

1 Heat the oil in a Dutch oven or large deep skillet over medium-high heat. Stir in the bell peppers, onion, and salt. Cook, stirring occasionally, until the mixture is barely softened and starting to char in places, 7 to 10 minutes.

2 Meanwhile, set up a large bowl of ice and water for an ice bath.

3 Reduce the heat to medium-low. Stir in the vinegar, anchovies, and pepper flakes (if using) and cook until the liquid is totally absorbed and the anchovies have melted (capers will not melt), another 4 to 7 minutes. Remove the mixture from the heat, scrape into a medium bowl, and set in the ice bath. Let cool to room temperature, about 30 minutes. If not baking the galette immediately, transfer the mixture to an airtight container and refrigerate for up to 2 days.

4 When you're ready to bake, preheat the oven to 425°F (220°C) with a rack positioned in the center. Line a sheet pan with parchment paper.

5 Roll the dough into a round or rectangle and set it on the lined sheet pan using the Basic Method (page 34).

Recipe continues

SERVES 4 TO 6

3 tablespoons (40 g) olive oil

1½ pounds (680 g) red, orange, and/or yellow bell peppers (about 3), stemmed and sliced ½ inch (13 mm) thick

1 medium red or yellow onion (6 ounces/160 g), sliced ¼ inch (6 mm) thick

½ teaspoon Diamond Crystal or ¼ teaspoon Morton kosher salt, plus more to taste

¼ cup (55 g) red wine vinegar

5 oil-packed anchovy fillets, or 2 tablespoons brined capers

½ teaspoon red pepper flakes (optional)

1 standard disk A Good Crust (page 27)

One 15-ounce (425 g) can butter or cannellini beans, drained and rinsed, or 1½ cups (250 g) cooked gigante, Royal Corona, or large lima beans

3 garlic cloves, finely grated

Freshly ground black pepper

Egg wash: 1 large egg, beaten

6 Stir the beans and garlic into the bell pepper mixture and season with salt and black pepper to taste. Spoon the bell pepper mixture into the crust, leaving a 2-inch (5 cm) border. Fold the edges of the crust over the filling toward the center, overlapping and pleating as desired. Freeze the galette on the sheet pan for 10 minutes.

7 Remove the galette from the freezer and brush the egg wash over the exposed crust.

8 Bake until the crust is starting to turn golden, 12 to 15 minutes. Reduce the oven temperature to 375°F (190°C) and continue to bake until the filling is starting to brown and the crust is deeply golden brown, another 35 to 45 minutes, rotating the sheet pan front to back halfway through.

9 Remove the galette from the oven and cool, uncovered, for 15 minutes or up to 2 hours.

10 Slice and serve.

Leftovers can be stored in an airtight container in the refrigerator for up to 3 days. Reheat on a sheet pan in a 350°F (180°C) oven until warmed through, about 10 minutes.

CRUST VARIATION OPTION: Whole Wheat (page 39)

SUMMER SQUASH AND ANY-HERB PESTO

SERVES 4 TO 6

1½ pounds (680 g) mixed summer squash and/or zucchini, sliced ⅛ inch (3 mm) thick

6 tablespoons (80 g) olive oil

½ teaspoon Diamond Crystal or ¼ teaspoon Morton kosher salt, plus more to taste

2 cups packed (90 g) mixed herb leaves and tender stems, such as basil, cilantro, parsley, and/or dill

½ cup (50 g) finely grated Parmesan cheese

⅓ cup (40 g) roughly chopped toasted nuts or seeds such as almonds, walnuts, sunflower seeds, or pumpkin seeds

4 garlic cloves

Freshly ground black pepper

1 standard disk A Good Crust (page 27)

Egg wash: 1 large egg, beaten

Flaky sea salt

Red pepper flakes (optional), for sprinkling

Lemon wedges, for serving

There is no better way to honor summer squash at its peak than to scatter it over freshly made pesto in a galette. You'll most often see basil in the pounded sauce, but cilantro, parsley, and dill can be used as well. And since we're going off-script with the herbs, when it comes to nuts, pine are traditional, but feel free to grab whatever's on hand: almonds, walnuts, even sunflower seeds. (That said, if you happen to have a pignoli nut budget, you should certainly use them, and please invite me over.) If you're in a rush, use a scant 1 cup (about 230 g) of store-bought pesto, even a vegan variety if you'd prefer no cheese.

1 In a large bowl, combine the squash, 1 tablespoon of the oil, and the kosher salt. Let sit for at least 10 minutes to draw out some moisture while you make the pesto.

2 In a food processor, combine the herbs, Parmesan, nuts, garlic, a couple of big pinches of kosher salt, and lots of black pepper. Pulse a few times until very finely chopped. With the motor running, slowly drizzle in 4 tablespoons of the oil until the mixture is smooth, stopping to stir or scrape down the bowl as needed if it gets stuck. (Alternatively, make the pesto with a mortar and pestle.) Season with more kosher salt to taste (it should be very garlicky and well seasoned; the flavor will mellow as it bakes).

3 Preheat the oven to 425°F (220°C) with a rack positioned in the center. Line a sheet pan with parchment paper.

4 Roll the dough into a round or rectangle and set it on the lined sheet pan using the Basic Method (page 34).

5 Spread the pesto over the crust, leaving a 2-inch (5 cm) border. Leaving any excess liquid in the bowl, arrange the squash in fanned-out bundles or rows, overlapping. Fold the edges of the crust over the filling toward the center, overlapping and pleating as desired. Freeze the galette on the sheet pan for 10 minutes.

6 Remove the galette from the freezer and brush the egg wash over the exposed crust. Drizzle the remaining 1 tablespoon oil over the filling.

7 Bake until the crust is starting to turn golden, 12 to 15 minutes. Reduce the oven temperature to 375°F (190°C) and continue to bake until the filling is starting to brown and the crust is deeply golden brown, another 40 to 50 minutes, rotating the sheet pan front to back halfway through.

8 Remove the galette from the oven and cool, uncovered, for 15 minutes or up to 2 hours.

9 Sprinkle flaky sea salt and pepper flakes (if using) over the galette. Slice and serve, with lemon wedges for squeezing over.

Leftovers can be stored in an airtight container in the refrigerator for up to 3 days. Reheat on a sheet pan in a 350°F (180°C) oven until warmed through, about 10 minutes.

CRUST VARIATION OPTIONS: Whole Wheat (page 39), Buckwheat (page 39)

GREENS, BRASSICAS, AND ALLIUMS

Leek and Sour Cream "Quiche"
186

Scallion and Asparagus with Miso
188

Cottage Cheesy Greens
with Chili Crisp
192

Smoky Cabbage and Chorizo
195

Sticky Onion with Anchovies
and Black Olives
198

Spiced Cauliflower,
Chickpeas, and Dates
201

I've never been one of those people who turn up their nose at eating leafy greens or brassicas (cabbage! cauliflower! broccoli!). When seasoned with enough fat, salt, and acid, any vegetable can be downright desirable. Just imagine them tossed with creamy cheese or a spicy condiment and baked into pastry. The bitterness of leafy greens tempers the richness of A Good Crust, often making quite the delightful accompaniment to a large-format protein. When roasted, brassicas go mild in flavor and tender in texture, complementing the strong flavors they're tossed with and adding heft to the galette.

Alliums shine in a pastry, too. Garlic, onion, shallot, or leek can improve the flavor of pretty much any dish, especially those with bitter greens. But let's be honest, sometimes we need to skip all the other vegetables and just rejoice in the gift that is caramelized onions in a buttery crust, adorned with an anchovy (or ten). We have that here, too.

LEEK AND SOUR CREAM "QUICHE"

SERVES 4 TO 6

9 ounces (255 g) leeks (2 to 3 small), white and light-green parts only, trimmed and sliced into rounds about ⅛ inch (3 mm) thick (about 3 cups)

4 large eggs

½ cup (115 g) sour cream

½ cup (50 g) finely grated Parmesan, pecorino, or Gruyère cheese

2 garlic cloves, grated

1 tablespoon all-purpose flour

½ teaspoon baking powder

1 teaspoon Diamond Crystal or ½ teaspoon Morton kosher salt

½ teaspoon freshly ground black pepper

Pinch of ground turmeric (optional)

Cooking spray or vegetable oil, for the pan

1 standard disk A Good Crust (page 27)

Quiche is a filling, affordable dish that needs little to no accompaniment to be an entire meal. So let's give it the galette treatment, shall we? To avoid the dreaded soggy bottom, most quiche crusts are blind-baked; as a galette, it's totally unnecessary. When baked in a tart pan with a slightly less liquidy custard, it winds up crisp from top to bottom, with a set but still creamy filling.

As for the filling, rings of leek provide the subtle sharpness we know and love about alliums, and unlike other produce often found in quiche (looking at you, spinach, mushrooms, and zucchini) require no precooking or squeezing to soften or release excess water.

NOTES: *If you don't have the patience to wash leeks, swap in 3 cups (about 255 g) sliced scallions, shallots, or onions, and skip the first step.*

The turmeric adds a pop of yellow color to this fairly beige filling—if you don't have any, just skip it.

Remember to lift the pan by its sides to avoid accidentally pushing out the removable bottom. To make your life easier, freeze the galette on a second sheet pan, tray, or cutting board before transferring it to the preheated sheet pan in the oven.

To unmold the galette, turn a medium bowl upside down and place the tart pan on top—the bowl will push up the removable bottom, separating the pan's wall while supporting the galette. Slide the galette onto a serving plate or cutting board (use a large offset or wide spatula to help if need be), then slice.

1 Place the leeks in a medium bowl of water, breaking up the rounds to allow water to clean dirt from its layers. Let sit for 10 minutes, then drain. Continue to soak and drain until the water runs clear, then dry on kitchen towels.

2 In a medium bowl, whisk together 3 of the eggs, the sour cream, half of the Parmesan, and the garlic until smooth. Whisk in the flour, baking powder, salt, pepper, and turmeric (if using).

3 Preheat the oven to 425°F (220°C) with a rack positioned in the center. Place a sheet pan in the oven to preheat.

4 Grease a 9- or 10-inch (23 or 25 cm) tart pan with a removable bottom or springform pan with cooking spray. Roll the dough into a round and fit it into the pan using the Pan Method (page 36).

5 Scatter the remaining half of the Parmesan over the base of the crust, then scatter over the leeks. Pour over the egg mixture. Twist and pleat the edges of the crust over the filling. Freeze the galette for 10 minutes (place the tart pan on another sheet pan to avoid touching the removable bottom).

6 In a small bowl, beat the remaining egg to make an egg wash. Remove the galette from the freezer and brush the egg wash over the exposed crust.

7 Place the tart pan on the preheated sheet pan in the oven. Bake until the crust is starting to turn golden, 12 to 15 minutes. Reduce the oven temperature to 375°F (190°C) and continue to bake until the crust is golden brown, the filling has puffed, and the top has started to take on color, another 30 to 35 minutes, rotating the sheet pan front to back halfway through. If the leeks start to look charred before 30 minutes, tent the exposed filling with foil and continue to bake.

8 Remove the galette from the oven and cool, uncovered, for 25 minutes or up to 2 hours before unmolding. Slice and serve.

Leftovers can be stored in an airtight container in the refrigerator for up to 2 days. Reheat on a sheet pan in a 350°F (180°C) oven until warmed through, about 10 minutes.

SPECIAL EQUIPMENT:
9- or 10-inch (23 or 25 cm) tart pan with a removable bottom or springform pan

CRUST VARIATION OPTIONS: Whole Wheat (page 39), Buckwheat (page 39), Peppery (page 40)

SERVE WITH: Garlicky Yogurt (page 43), harissa paste

SCALLION AND ASPARAGUS WITH MISO

SERVES 6 TO 8

2 tablespoons white miso

2 tablespoons unseasoned rice vinegar

1 tablespoon toasted sesame oil, plus more for serving

1 tablespoon yuzu koshō or sriracha (see Notes)

1½ pounds (680 g) asparagus, woody bottoms trimmed, halved lengthwise if large

1 bunch (175 g) scallions (6 to 8), trimmed and halved lengthwise if large, or 4 to 6 spring onions, trimmed and quartered lengthwise

1 XL disk A Good Crust (page 27)

Egg wash: 1 large egg, beaten

Black or white sesame seeds

CRUST VARIATION OPTION: Whole Wheat (page 39)

Come spring, it's impossible to resist the asparagus. Head to the market and find them snuggled together in bunches with thick rubber bands. Tuck a few into your tote bag and head over to the alliums. Scallions should be plentiful, but if you can get your hands on spring onions, use them instead. The early onions have reedlike tails and round bulbs, and are sometimes streaked with purple. Asparagus and scallions tend to be about the same size, but depending on the variety, either can be as slim as a mechanical pencil or chubby as a broad Sharpie. Any and all sizes will bake up delightfully, but for easier slicing it's best to keep everything thinner.

NOTES: *If you can't find yuzu koshō, the spicy-floral Japanese paste of red or green chiles and yuzu, add the grated zest of 1 lemon and 1 lime (if you have them) along with 1 tablespoon sriracha—they'll contribute some comparable citrusy notes.*

For an extra-crisp slab-galette crust, place a sheet pan in the oven as it preheats. Prepare the galette as written, freezing it on a second sheet pan. After brushing the galette with egg wash, remove the hot sheet pan from the oven and place it on a heatproof surface (like your stove). Bring the chilled galette nearby, carefully lift it by the parchment paper, and place it on the preheated sheet pan. Bake as directed.

1 Preheat the oven to 425°F (220°C) with a rack positioned in the center. Line a sheet pan with parchment paper.

2 In a large bowl, whisk together the miso, vinegar, sesame oil, and yuzu koshō. Gently toss with the asparagus and scallions to coat.

3 Roll the dough out using the Slab Method (page 36) and set it on the lined sheet pan.

4 Arrange the asparagus mixture over the crust, leaving a 2½-inch (6 cm) border. Fold the edges of the crust over the filling toward the center to make a rectangle, overlapping and pleating as desired. Freeze the galette on the sheet pan for 10 minutes.

5 Remove the galette from the freezer and brush the egg wash over the exposed crust. Sprinkle the crust with sesame seeds.

6 Bake until the crust is starting to turn golden, 12 to 15 minutes. Reduce the oven temperature to 375°F (190°C) and continue to bake until the filling is browned and the crust is deeply golden brown, another 40 to 50 minutes, rotating the sheet pan front to back halfway through.

7 Remove the galette from the oven and cool, uncovered, for 25 minutes or up to 8 hours.

8 Drizzle with a little more sesame oil, slice, and serve.

Leftovers can be stored at room temperature, loosely covered, for up to 24 hours or in the refrigerator for up to 2 days. Reheat on a sheet pan in a 350°F (180°C) oven until warmed through, about 10 minutes.

COTTAGE CHEESY GREENS WITH CHILI CRISP

SERVES 4 TO 6

3 tablespoons (40 g) olive oil

12 ounces (340 g) leafy greens (about 1 small bunch), such as kale, mustard greens, or Swiss chard, stems removed, leaves roughly torn

12 ounces (340 g) broccoli rabe (about 1 bunch), roughly chopped

¾ cup (175 g) full-fat cottage cheese

½ cup (50 g) finely grated Parmesan or pecorino cheese

2 tablespoons chili crisp (any heat level), plus more for serving

1 bunch (175 g) scallions (6 to 8) or 1 small leek, washed, trimmed, and thinly sliced

Diamond Crystal or Morton kosher salt

Cooking spray or vegetable oil, for the pan

1 standard disk A Good Crust (page 27)

Egg wash: 1 large egg, beaten

Lemon wedges, for serving

Classic creamed greens get a makeover into a substantial, just-spicy-enough galette you'll want to make all winter long. Wilt your favorite dark leafy greens with bitter broccoli rabe, and swap the traditional heavy cream for full-fat cottage cheese and a grated firm cheese, which brings a welcome tang and saltiness to the mix. A good pour of chili crisp lends rich warmth to each bite.

1 Set up a large bowl of ice and water for an ice bath. Heat the oil in a Dutch oven or large deep skillet over medium heat. Working in batches if needed, stir in the leafy greens and broccoli rabe. Cook, stirring occasionally, until wilted, 3 to 5 minutes. Remove the greens from the heat, scrape into a medium bowl, and set in the ice bath. Let cool to room temperature, about 15 minutes. If not baking the galette immediately, transfer the mixture to an airtight container and refrigerate for up to 24 hours.

2 Meanwhile, in a large bowl, stir together the cottage cheese, Parmesan, and chili crisp until combined.

3 Add the wilted greens to the cottage cheese mixture along with the scallions and salt to taste (the amount will depend on the saltiness of your cheese and chili crisp).

4 Preheat the oven to 425°F (220°C) with a rack positioned in the center. Place a sheet pan in the oven to preheat.

Recipe continues

5 Grease a 9- or 10-inch (23 or 25 cm) cast-iron skillet, pie plate, or cake pan with cooking spray. Roll the dough into a round and fit it into the vessel using the Pan Method (page 36).

6 Pour the greens mixture into the crust. Fold the edges of the crust over the filling toward the center, overlapping and pleating as desired. Freeze the galette for 10 minutes.

7 Remove the galette from the freezer and brush the egg wash over the exposed crust.

8 Place the skillet on the preheated sheet pan in the oven. Bake until the crust is starting to turn golden, 12 to 15 minutes. Reduce the oven temperature to 375°F (190°C) and continue to bake until the filling is starting to brown and the crust is deeply golden and pulling away from the edges of the pan, 40 to 50 minutes, rotating the sheet pan front to back halfway through.

9 Remove the galette from the oven and cool, uncovered, for 25 minutes or up to 2 hours.

10 Slice and serve, with lemon wedges to squeeze over, and more chili crisp if you'd like.

Leftovers can be stored in an airtight container in the refrigerator for up to 2 days. Reheat on a sheet pan in a 350°F (180°C) oven until warmed through, about 10 minutes.

HOW TO MAKE JAMMY EGGS

Drop room-temperature eggs into boiling water for 7 minutes, chill in ice water for 5 minutes, then peel.

SMOKY CABBAGE AND CHORIZO

Smoky fresh chorizo bleeds a fiery-orange oil as it cooks. To make the most of this in a galette, start with a base of caramelized cabbage; it's tough enough to stand up to the rich, spicy sausage. Finish like you would a good taco, with chopped cilantro, diced onion (I prefer white, but whatever you used in the filling will work), Cotija cheese or queso fresco, and lots of lime.

NOTE: *Fresh chorizo, sometimes labeled Mexican chorizo, is raw and uncured. If you can't find it, use hot Italian sausage (not the same but still tasty). Or DIY: Mix 8 ounces (225 g) ground pork (or Impossible/Beyond Beef) with 2 teaspoons hot smoked paprika, 1 teaspoon garlic powder, ½ teaspoon chili powder, and ½ teaspoon Diamond Crystal or ¼ teaspoon Morton kosher salt.*

1 Heat the oil in a Dutch oven or large deep skillet over medium-high heat. Stir in the cabbage, sliced onions, and salt. It will look like way too much cabbage, but it'll cook down. Cook, stirring occasionally, until the mixture is slightly softened, 8 to 10 minutes. If the mixture starts to singe, reduce the heat and continue cooking.

2 Reduce the heat to medium, stir in the adobo sauce and chipotle pepper, if using, and use your spoon to smash it down as it cooks. Continue cooking, stirring occasionally, until the mixture is slightly more softened and darkened in color, another 8 to 10 minutes.

3 Meanwhile, set up a large bowl of ice and water for an ice bath.

Recipe continues

SERVES 4 TO 6

3 tablespoons (40 g) olive oil

1 pound (455 g) red or green cabbage (about ½ large), thinly sliced

1 pound (455 g) red, white, or yellow onions (about 4 medium), thinly sliced, plus more, diced, for serving

1½ teaspoons Diamond Crystal or ¾ teaspoon Morton kosher salt

2 tablespoons adobo sauce from canned chipotle peppers, or tomato paste

1 canned chipotle pepper in adobo sauce, or ½ teaspoon red pepper flakes (optional)

1 standard disk A Good Crust (page 27)

Egg wash: 1 large egg, beaten

1½ teaspoons cumin seeds (optional)

8 ounces (225 g) fresh chorizo, any casings removed

Chopped fresh cilantro, for serving

Crumbled Cotija or queso fresco (optional), for serving

Lime wedges, for serving

4 Remove the cabbage mixture from the heat, scrape into a medium bowl, and set in the ice bath. Let cool to room temperature, about 30 minutes. If not baking the galette immediately, transfer the mixture to an airtight container and refrigerate for up to 24 hours.

5 Preheat the oven to 425°F (220°C) with a rack positioned in the center. Line a sheet pan with parchment paper.

6 Roll the dough into a round and set it on the lined sheet pan using the Basic Method (page 34).

7 Spoon the cabbage mixture into the crust, leaving a 2-inch (5 cm) border. Fold the edges of the crust over the filling toward the center, overlapping and pleating as desired. Freeze the galette on the sheet pan for 10 minutes.

8 Remove the galette from the freezer and brush the egg wash over the exposed crust. Sprinkle the entire galette, including the crust, with cumin seeds (if using).

9 Bake until the crust is starting to turn golden, 12 to 15 minutes. Reduce the oven temperature to 375°F (190°C) and continue to bake until the crust has turned a deeper brown, 20 to 25 minutes.

10 Remove the galette from the oven and carefully crumble the chorizo over the filling in ½-inch (13 mm) pieces. Return the galette to the oven and continue to bake until the sausage is cooked through and the crust is deeply golden brown, another 20 to 25 minutes.

11 Remove the galette from the oven and cool, uncovered, for 15 minutes or up to 2 hours.

12 Top with cilantro, diced onion, and Cotija (if using). Slice and serve, with lime wedges for squeezing.

Best eaten day-of. Leftovers can be stored in an airtight container in the refrigerator for up to 2 days; if you don't mind wilting the toppings, reheat on a sheet pan in a 350°F (180°C) oven until warmed through, about 10 minutes.

CRUST VARIATION OPTION: Cornmeal (page 39)

STICKY ONION WITH ANCHOVIES AND BLACK OLIVES

SERVES 4 TO 6

SERVES 4 TO 6

3 tablespoons (40 g) olive oil

2½ pounds (1.1 kg) red or yellow onions (about 7 medium), halved lengthwise and thinly sliced

6 garlic cloves, thinly sliced

2 dried bay leaves

2 tablespoons fresh thyme leaves

1 teaspoon Diamond Crystal or ½ teaspoon Morton kosher salt, plus more to taste

2 to 3 tablespoons dry vermouth or white wine vinegar

1 tablespoon tomato paste

1 teaspoon piment d'Espelette (see Note), or ½ teaspoon red pepper flakes

1 standard disk A Good Crust (page 27)

Egg wash: 1 large egg, beaten

Oil-packed anchovy fillets, drained, for topping

Pitted kalamata or Niçoise olives, for topping

Reminiscent of the pissaladière you'd find in the South of France, this galette is the ultimate play on sweet and salty. Cook down a mountain of onions with a splash of vermouth until they've caramelized sweet and dark, then spoon into the crust. Before cutting, arrange the best anchovies and black olives you can find over the top in whatever pattern pleases you.

NOTE: *Piment d'Espelette, or Espelette pepper, popular in Basque cuisine, offers a smoky-sweet heat without overpowering a dish.*

1 Heat the oil in a Dutch oven or large deep skillet over medium-high heat. Stir in the onions, garlic, bay leaves, thyme, and salt. It will look like way too many onions, but they'll cook down. Cook, stirring occasionally, until the onions are soft and lightly golden brown, 30 to 40 minutes. If you find the onions are looking charred or fried, add a splash of water and reduce the heat to medium.

2 Stir in 2 tablespoons of the vermouth, letting the liquid loosen any onions that are stuck on the bottom of the pot (add up to an additional tablespoon if any are really stuck). Stir in the tomato paste, piment d'Espelette, and a pinch of salt. Continue to cook, stirring often, until the liquid is totally absorbed, another 8 to 10 minutes.

3 Meanwhile, set up a large bowl of ice and water for an ice bath.

4 Remove the onions from the heat, scrape into a medium bowl set in the ice bath, and let cool to room temperature,

CRUST VARIATION OPTIONS: Whole Wheat (page 39), Buckwheat (page 39)

SERVE WITH: Before-dinner drinks, salted tomatoes, marinated lentils

about 30 minutes. At this point, if you taste the onions, you should find them in need of a pinch of salt—don't add any (the topping is salty)! Remove and discard the bay leaves. If not baking the galette immediately, transfer to an airtight container and refrigerate for up to 2 days.

5 Preheat the oven to 425°F (220°C) with a rack positioned in the center. Line a sheet pan with parchment paper.

6 Roll the dough into a rectangle and set it on the lined sheet pan using the Basic Method (page 34).

7 Spoon the onion mixture into the crust, leaving a 1½-inch (4 cm) border. Fold the edges of the crust over the filling toward the center to make a rectangle, overlapping and pleating as desired. Freeze the galette on the sheet pan for 10 minutes.

8 Remove the galette from the freezer and brush the egg wash over the exposed crust.

9 Bake until the crust is starting to turn golden, 12 to 15 minutes. Reduce the oven temperature to 375°F (190°C) and continue to bake until the crust is deeply golden brown, another 25 to 30 minutes, rotating the sheet pan front to back halfway through. (If the filling produces an air bubble at any point, carefully poke it with a paring knife to release.)

10 Remove the galette from the oven and cool, uncovered, for 15 minutes or up to 8 hours.

11 Arrange the anchovies and olives over the top—diagonal rows or a checkerboard is fun. Slice and serve.

Leftovers can be stored in an airtight container in the refrigerator for up to 3 days. Reheat on a sheet pan in a 350°F (180°C) oven until warmed through, about 10 minutes.

VARIATION

Play on the Niçoise tuna sandwich pan bagnat by topping the cooled galette with flaked oil-packed tuna, sliced tomatoes, and jammy eggs (page 194). Season with salt and black pepper, then shower with basil and lemon juice.

SPICED CAULIFLOWER, CHICKPEAS, AND DATES

Rooting through the kitchen to find a head of cauliflower and a can of chickpeas may not sound like the start of the most exciting meal, but just you wait. Toss them with a garlicky spiced oil (pantry staples!), pleat around A Good Crust (from the freezer!), and you might as well throw a dinner party. And if you're not yet clued in to the delight that is roasted dates, I'm so excited for you—you never forget your first time.

1 In a large bowl, stir together the oil, garlic, cumin seeds, sesame seeds, mustard seeds, Aleppo pepper, and salt. Slice the cauliflower into slabs ¼ inch (6 mm) thick, letting any smaller pieces naturally separate, then cut into bite-size pieces. If using cabbage, slice through the core into 1-inch (2.5 cm) wedges. Gently toss the cauliflower, chickpeas, and dates in the large bowl to coat in the spiced oil.

2 Preheat the oven to 425°F (220°C) with a rack positioned in the center. Line a sheet pan with parchment paper.

3 Roll the dough into a round and set it on the lined sheet pan using the Basic Method (page 34).

4 Arrange the filling over the crust, leaving a 2-inch (5 cm) border. Fold the edges of the the filling toward the center, overlapping and pleating as desired. Freeze the galette on the sheet pan for 10 minutes.

5 Remove the galette from the freezer and brush the egg wash over the exposed crust.

Recipe continues

SERVES 4 TO 6

¼ cup (50 g) olive oil

3 garlic cloves, grated

2 teaspoons cumin seeds

2 teaspoons white sesame seeds

2 teaspoons yellow mustard seeds

2 teaspoons Aleppo pepper, or ½ teaspoon red pepper flakes

1 teaspoon Diamond Crystal or ½ teaspoon Morton kosher salt, plus more as needed

12 ounces (345 g) cauliflower, broccoli, Romanesco, or savoy cabbage (about 1 medium head)

One 15-ounce (425 g) can chickpeas or white beans, such as cannellini or navy, drained and rinsed

4 to 6 (70 g) pitted Medjool dates, torn into pieces

1 standard disk A Good Crust (page 27)

Egg wash: 1 large egg, beaten

Torn mint leaves, for serving

6 Bake until the crust is starting to turn golden, 12 to 15 minutes. Reduce the oven temperature to 375°F (190°C) and continue to bake until the filling is browned and the crust is deeply golden brown, another 40 to 50 minutes, rotating the sheet pan front to back halfway through.

7 Remove the galette from the oven and cool, uncovered, for 15 minutes or up to 8 hours.

8 Slice and serve, topped with mint.

Without the mint, leftovers can be stored in an airtight container in the refrigerator for up to 3 days. Reheat on a sheet pan in a 350°F (180°C) oven until warmed through, about 10 minutes.

CRUST VARIATION OPTION: Whole Wheat (page 39)

SERVE WITH: Zingy Tahini (page 43) or Garlicky Yogurt (page 43)

PANTRY
STAPLES

Cheesy Ham and Eggs
208

Pepperoni Pizza
210

Rotisserie Chicken, Potato, and Chèvre
213

Marinated Artichoke and Tomato
216

White Pie with Salad
(and Maybe Mortadella)
219

Lemony Spinach and Rice
222

Chopped Mushroom and Kimchi
225

It may seem counterintuitive, but some of the best savory galettes are made with items found in the cans, containers, and jars that you keep in your pantry. Kimchi, marinated artichokes, rice, sun-dried tomatoes, chickpeas, and marinara sauce all make excellent galette components—and I bet you have some of these on hand already. Prepared meats fit in delightfully as well: Rotisserie chicken, pepperoni, mortadella, and deli ham, come on down. But these galettes aren't devoid of produce; they simply shine a light on the less-popular varieties. The brown, the frozen, the passed up for whatever's in peak season: Mushrooms, spinach, arugula, and tiny tomatoes are the real backbone of the savory produce economy.

Say you're cooking at a rental and there's only one (limited) grocery store in town. Or you're trying to save a little money on a holiday dinner by pulling back on the flashy produce. Or you want to have a pizza party without delivery. Or you're just feeling too lazy to shop and want to cobble together a meal from what's already in the kitchen. These are the galettes for you.

CHEESY HAM AND EGGS

MAKES 4 SMALL GALETTES

1 standard disk A Good Crust (page 27), preferably the Buckwheat variation

2 tablespoons Dijon mustard, plus more for serving

1⅓ cups (145 g) shredded Gruyère cheese

Freshly ground black pepper

4 ounces (115 g) thinly sliced ham, such as jambon de Paris or prosciutto cotto

5 large eggs

Cornichons, for serving

CRUST VARIATION OPTIONS: Whole Wheat (page 39), Buckwheat (page 39)

Ham and cheese are natural bedfellows; with a swipe of mustard and a just-set egg enrobed in pastry, the combination is irresistible. As a nod to Breton galettes complètes (which are actually crepes), use the nutty Buckwheat variation of A Good Crust. Of course, if you happen to already have a chilled disk of standard or Whole Wheat, don't let that stop you from baking. Instead of pleating the crust to make round galettes like other recipes that use the Tiny Method, this one calls for each dough round to be folded over the filling in quadrants to form squares, mimicking the shape of galettes complètes.

NOTES: *If you're not an egg fan, or don't feel like the extra work, feel free to skip the 4 eggs on top—the galettes will still be lovely.*

The recipe makes 4 small galettes but is easily doubled if you're serving a larger group: Bake on two sheet pans on racks positioned in the upper and lower thirds of the oven, and switch racks halfway through baking.

1 Preheat the oven to 375°F (190°C) with a rack positioned in the center. Line a sheet pan with parchment paper.

2 Roll out 4 dough rounds using the Tiny Method (page 36) and arrange evenly spaced on the lined sheet pan.

3 Brush about ½ tablespoon mustard in the center of each dough round, leaving a 2-inch (5 cm) border. Sprinkle about ⅓ cup (35 g) Gruyère over the mustard. Season with pepper. Place 1 ounce (28 g/1 to 2 slices) ham just over the cheese, tearing as needed, keeping it relatively flat.

4 Beat 1 of the eggs in a small bowl. Brush some beaten egg around the edge of each dough round, right up to the filling. Fold one edge of the crust over the filling toward the center, gently pressing the corners together to adhere where the egg-washed parts meet. Fold over the opposite edge of the crust, and repeat with the two remaining edges, gently pressing at each corner to seal (add additional egg wash as needed, and leave roughly 2 inches/5 cm of ham exposed) into little square packages. Freeze the galettes on the sheet pan for 15 minutes.

5 Remove the galettes from the freezer and brush more egg wash all over the exposed crust on each galette.

6 Bake until the crusts are golden brown, 25 to 30 minutes, rotating the sheet pan front to back halfway through. If any of the edges unfold during the first half of baking, you can use a butter knife to gently refold them when rotating the pan. The crust should look like it needs a bit more time in the oven.

7 While the galettes bake, prepare the remaining eggs: Crack 1 of the remaining eggs into a fine-mesh sieve placed over a medium bowl. Let the very runny outer egg white—but not all of it—run through the sieve: This will help the eggs fit easily into the galette and set more evenly in the oven. Place the strained egg in a small bowl. Repeat with the remaining eggs. (Discard the excess egg white or save for egg wash; see page 18.)

8 Remove the galettes from the oven. Use a spoon to gently press down on the ham, then carefully pour an egg into the center of each galette. Return to the oven and bake until the egg whites are cooked through, the yolks are set to your liking, and the crusts have taken on a bit more color, another 8 to 12 minutes. Remove the galettes from the oven and cool for 5 minutes.

9 Serve warm, with cornichons and more mustard.

Best eaten within 2 hours. Leftovers can be stored in an airtight container in the refrigerator for up to 24 hours; if you don't mind slightly overcooking the eggs, reheat on a sheet pan in a 350°F (180°C) oven until warmed through, about 10 minutes.

PEPPERONI PIZZA

SERVES 4 TO 6

1 XL disk A Good Crust (page 27)

3 cups (330 g) shredded low-moisture mozzarella cheese

1 cup (100 g) finely grated Parmesan cheese, plus more for serving

1½ cups (375 g) jarred marinara sauce

½ cup (40 g) pepperoni (about 20 slices)

Egg wash: 1 large egg, beaten

Sliced pepperoncini (optional), for serving

Red pepper flakes and/or dried oregano, for serving

SERVE WITH: A giant salad

A galette is decidedly not pizza, but you can treat one like the other. A Good Crust lacks pizza dough's tangy chew but of course makes up for it in buttery crispness, and is just as pleasant a bed for tomato sauce and cheese. Supermarket staples like shredded mozzarella, grated Parmesan, and jarred marinara make this a meal that's easily tossed together wherever you happen to be baking.

This is made with an XL disk of A Good Crust, but you'll find that it quickly disappears with 4 to 6 eaters. If you only have a standard disk of dough on hand, just halve the rest of the ingredients. And don't be shy about switching out the pepperoni for other beloved pizza toppings: Peppers, onions, mushrooms, olives, and anchovies (to name just a few) are very welcome here.

NOTE: *For an extra-crisp slab-galette crust, place a sheet pan in the oven as it preheats. Prepare the galette as written, freezing it on a second sheet pan. After brushing the galette with egg wash, remove the hot sheet pan from the oven and place it on a heatproof surface (like your stove). Bring the chilled galette nearby, carefully lift it by the parchment paper, and place it on the preheated sheet pan. Bake as directed.*

1 Preheat the oven to 425°F (220°C) with a rack positioned in the center. Line a sheet pan with parchment paper.

2 Roll out the dough using the Slab Method (page 36) and set it on the lined sheet pan.

Recipe continues

3 Sprinkle the mozzarella over the crust, leaving a 2-inch (5 cm) border. Sprinkle the Parmesan over the mozzarella. Dollop spoonfuls of the marinara over the cheese. Top with the pepperoni. Fold the edges of the crust over the filling toward the center, overlapping and pleating as desired to make a rectangle. Freeze the galette on the sheet pan for 10 minutes.

4 Remove the galette from the freezer and brush the egg wash over the exposed crust.

5 Bake until the crust is starting to turn golden, 12 to 15 minutes. Reduce the oven temperature to 375°F (190°C) and continue to bake until the cheese has melted and is starting to brown and the crust is deeply golden brown, another 30 to 35 minutes, rotating the sheet pan front to back halfway through. If the cheese starts to get very dark in spots before 30 minutes, tent the exposed filling with foil and continue to bake.

6 Remove the galette from the oven and cool, uncovered, for 15 minutes or up to 2 hours.

7 Top with pepperoncini (if using), and sprinkle with pepper flakes and/or oregano. Slice and serve.

Leftovers can be stored in an airtight container in the refrigerator for up to 3 days. Reheat on a sheet pan in a 350°F (180°C) oven until warmed through, about 10 minutes.

ROTISSERIE CHICKEN, POTATO, AND CHÈVRE

If chicken pot pie went on a French vacation, I imagine it'd come back looking something like this. Shredded rotisserie chicken and crushed potatoes are dressed with Dijon mustard and wine, then get cozy with an herb-spiked chèvre. A meal unto itself, it's perfect to make for a picnic (though no one will mind if you serve slices alongside salad or some crunchy veg) and is just as good at room temperature as it is hot from the oven. With galettes like these, who needs a sandwich?

1 In a medium pot, combine the potatoes, 2 tablespoons Diamond Crystal or 1 tablespoon Morton kosher salt, and water to cover by 2 inches (5 cm). Bring to a boil over high heat. Reduce the heat to medium-high and cook until the potatoes are fork-tender, about 12 minutes. Drain the potatoes in a colander, rinse with cold water, and let cool. (If not baking the galette today, refrigerate the potatoes in an airtight container for up to 1 week.)

2 Grate the zest of the lemon into a small bowl; set the lemon aside. Add the chèvre, thyme, tarragon, ¼ teaspoon Diamond Crystal or ⅛ teaspoon Morton kosher salt, and a few grinds of pepper and fold and smash with a spatula to combine. Refrigerate until you're ready to add it to the galette (or in an airtight container for up to 2 days).

3 In a large bowl, whisk together the mustard, wine, and oil.

4 When the potatoes are cool to touch, gently crush them with your hands or the bottom of a cup and place in the large

SERVES 4 TO 6

- 12 ounces (340 g) tiny creamer or fingerling potatoes, scrubbed
- 2 tablespoons plus ¼ teaspoon Diamond Crystal or 1 tablespoon plus ⅛ teaspoon Morton kosher salt, plus more to taste
- 1 lemon
- 6 ounces (170 g) chèvre
- 2 tablespoons fresh thyme leaves, finely chopped
- 2 tablespoons fresh tarragon leaves, finely chopped
- Freshly ground black pepper
- 3 tablespoons (45 g) Dijon mustard
- 3 tablespoons (45 g) dry white wine or vermouth (or fresh lemon juice)
- 2 tablespoons olive oil
- 2 cups (300 g) shredded rotisserie (or any cooked) chicken
- 1 small red onion (4½ ounces/ 125 g), thinly sliced (about ¾ cup)
- Cooking spray or vegetable oil, for the pan
- 1 standard disk A Good Crust (page 27)
- Egg wash: 1 large egg, beaten

bowl with the mustard mixture. Fold in the chicken, onion, and the chèvre mixture (broken into small clumps) until combined. Season with salt and pepper to taste.

5 Preheat the oven to 425°F (220°C) with a rack positioned in the center. Place a sheet pan in the oven to preheat.

6 Grease a 9- or 10-inch (23 or 25 cm) cast-iron skillet, pie plate, or cake pan with cooking spray. Roll the dough into a round and fit it into the vessel using the Pan Method (page 36).

7 Spoon the chicken mixture into the crust. Fold the edges of the crust over the filling toward the center, overlapping and pleating as desired. Freeze the galette for 10 minutes.

8 Remove the galette from the freezer and brush the egg wash over the exposed crust.

9 Place the skillet on the preheated sheet pan in the oven. Bake until the crust is starting to turn golden, 12 to 15 minutes. Reduce the oven temperature to 375°F (190°C) and continue to bake until the filling is browned and the crust is deeply golden brown, another 40 to 50 minutes, rotating the pan front to back halfway through.

10 Remove the galette from the oven and cool, uncovered, for 25 minutes or up to 2 hours.

11 Cut the reserved lemon into wedges. Slice the galette and serve with lemon wedges for squeezing.

Leftovers can be stored in an airtight container in the refrigerator for up to 2 days. Reheat on a sheet pan in a 350°F (180°C) oven until warmed through, about 10 minutes.

VARIATION
For a Buffalo wing–inspired version, swap in crumbled blue cheese for the chèvre; omit the thyme and tarragon; add ½ cup (50 g) sliced celery along with the chicken; and swap in store-bought Buffalo wing sauce for the mustard, with more for serving.

SPECIAL EQUIPMENT: 9- or 10-inch (23 or 25 cm) cast-iron skillet, metal or ceramic pie plate, or cake pan

CRUST VARIATION OPTIONS: Whole Wheat (page 39), Peppery (page 40)

SERVE WITH: The rest of the wine you opened to make the filling

MARINATED ARTICHOKE AND TOMATO

SERVES 4 TO 6

12 ounces (340 g) small tomatoes (about 2 heaping cups), such as cherry, grape, or Campari (halved or quartered if larger than 1½ inches/4 cm)

½ teaspoon Diamond Crystal or ¼ teaspoon Morton kosher salt, plus more to taste

One 14-ounce (400 g) can water-packed artichoke hearts, drained and quartered (see Note)

¾ cup (150 g) roughly chopped oil-packed sun-dried tomatoes (oil reserved)

4 garlic cloves, grated

2 tablespoons brined capers, drained

1 tablespoon dried oregano, or 2 tablespoons chopped fresh

1 tablespoon red wine vinegar

½ teaspoon red pepper flakes (optional)

Freshly ground black pepper

1 standard disk A Good Crust (page 27)

1 cup (110 g) shredded low-moisture mozzarella cheese

Egg wash: 1 large egg, beaten

If you've ever visited the prepared foods counter at a supermarket to load up on pints of brined, oiled, herbed vegetables and made that a meal, keep reading. This marinated artichoke and tomato number can be made even with the saddest winter tomatoes: Just stick with small ones, like Campari, cherry, grape, or on-the-vine, which are flavorful year-round. And notice those pops of sweetness? The dream of the '90s is alive and well in a jar of sun-dried tomatoes, offering a welcome addition to this acidic, fatty situation. PS: If you're not already on the canned-artichoke train, well, all aboard.

NOTE: *If buying artichoke hearts from a bulk container, you'll need 8½ ounces (240 g/5 to 7 hearts), drained.*

1 In a medium bowl, toss the fresh tomatoes with the salt. Spread out in a single layer, cut-side down, on paper towels or kitchen towels to drain. To the now-empty bowl, add the artichokes, sun-dried tomatoes, garlic, capers, oregano, vinegar, pepper flakes (if using), and lots of black pepper. Set aside to marinate for 20 minutes.

2 Preheat the oven to 425°F (220°C) with a rack positioned in the center. Line a sheet pan with parchment paper.

3 Roll the dough into a round or rectangle and set it on the lined sheet pan using the Basic Method (page 34).

4 Stir the fresh tomatoes and half of the mozzarella into the artichoke mixture. Season with more salt and/or black pepper to taste.

Recipe continues

CRUST VARIATION OPTIONS: Whole Wheat (page 39), Cornmeal (page 39)

5 Sprinkle the remaining mozzarella over the crust, leaving a 2-inch (5 cm) border. Pour the artichoke mixture over the cheese. Fold the edges of the crust over the filling toward the center, overlapping and pleating as desired. Freeze the galette on the sheet pan for 10 minutes.

6 Remove the galette from the freezer and brush the egg wash over the exposed crust. Drizzle 1 tablespoon of the reserved sun-dried tomato oil over the filling.

7 Bake until the crust is starting to turn golden, 12 to 15 minutes. Reduce the oven temperature to 375°F (190°C) and continue to bake until the filling is starting to brown and the crust is deeply golden brown, another 40 to 50 minutes, rotating the sheet pan front to back halfway through.

8 Remove the galette from the oven and cool, uncovered, for 15 minutes or up to 2 hours.

9 Slice and serve.

Leftovers can be stored in an airtight container in the refrigerator for up to 3 days. Reheat on a sheet pan in a 350°F (180°C) oven until warmed through, about 10 minutes.

WHITE PIE WITH SALAD
(AND MAYBE MORTADELLA)

Dinner guests will delight in this riff on pizza bianca (aka white pizza, or a pie sans tomato sauce). What's more, you can dress it up to serve your interests. Top the garlicky ricotta galette with just the salad; or, if you're a meat eater, first drape on a layer of mortadella. For a summery slant, scatter with very ripe wedges of fresh peach or plum, with or without the cured meat.

NOTE: *Make sure to use a ricotta that has some lightness to it (you should be able to stir it with no challenge straight from the fridge); if it's thick like cream cheese, use ½ cup (115 g) ricotta stirred with 2 or 3 tablespoons heavy cream until it's smooth and lighter, like Greek yogurt. The bottom crust may bake off slightly less crisp but will still taste great.*

1 Preheat the oven to 425°F (220°C) with a rack positioned in the center. Line a sheet pan with parchment paper.

2 In a small bowl, combine the ricotta, garlic, lemon zest, pepper, and kosher salt.

3 Roll the dough into a round and set it on the lined sheet pan using the Basic Method (page 34).

4 Spoon the ricotta mixture into the crust, leaving a 1-inch (2.5 cm) border. Scatter the mozzarella over the ricotta, then sprinkle the Parmesan over the mozzarella. Twist and crimp the crust border over itself to make a 1-inch (2.5 cm) border. (Alternatively, as for any other galette, fold the edges of the crust over the filling toward the center, overlapping and

SERVES 4 TO 6

Scant ¾ cup (170 g) whole-milk ricotta cheese

4 garlic cloves, grated

1 tablespoon grated lemon zest

½ teaspoon coarsely ground black pepper

¼ teaspoon Diamond Crystal or ⅛ teaspoon Morton kosher salt

1 standard disk A Good Crust (page 27)

6 ounces (170 g) low-moisture mozzarella cheese, sliced or torn into ⅛-inch-thick (3 mm) bite-size pieces

½ cup (50 g) finely grated Parmesan cheese

Egg wash: 1 large egg, beaten

4 ounces (115 g) thinly sliced mortadella or prosciutto (optional)

3 cups (30 g) baby arugula

Fresh lemon juice, for serving

Honey, for serving

Good extra-virgin olive oil, for serving

Flaky sea salt

pleating as desired.) Freeze the galette on the sheet pan for 10 minutes.

5 Remove the galette from the freezer and brush the egg wash over the exposed crust.

6 Bake until the crust is starting to turn golden, 12 to 15 minutes. Reduce the oven temperature to 375°F (190°C) and continue to bake until the filling is browned in spots and the crust is deeply golden brown, another 25 to 30 minutes, rotating the sheet pan front to back halfway through. If the cheese starts to get very dark in spots before 25 minutes, tent the exposed filling with foil and continue to bake.

7 Remove the galette from the oven and cool, uncovered, for 15 minutes or up to 2 hours.

8 If using, drape the mortadella over the surface of the galette. Top the galette with the arugula. Drizzle with lemon juice, honey, and a glug of oil to very lightly dress it, then sprinkle with flaky sea salt. Slice and serve.

Best eaten day-of.

LEMONY SPINACH AND RICE

MAKES 4 SMALL GALETTES

3 tablespoons (9 g) Diamond Crystal or 1½ tablespoons Morton kosher salt, plus more to taste

½ cup (90 g) basmati rice, rinsed until the water runs clear

One 10-ounce (285 g) package frozen spinach, thawed (about 2 cups)

4 garlic cloves, grated

¾ cup (125 g) cooked chickpeas (about half of a 15-ounce/425 g can, drained and rinsed)

¼ cup (40 g) golden raisins, dried tart cherries, or sweet cherries

⅓ cup (75 g) plain whole-milk yogurt

2 tablespoons olive oil

1 tablespoon grated lemon zest

2 tablespoons fresh lemon juice

Freshly ground black pepper

1 standard disk A Good Crust (page 27)

Egg wash: 1 large egg, beaten

Sliced or crumbled feta cheese, for serving

Fans of the Greek pilaf spanakorizo will swoon for these small-scale galettes. Chickpeas and dried fruit threaded through basmati rice and spinach add heft and sweetness; whole-milk yogurt binds the whole mess together. Make the filling a day ahead and you'll find assembly is a snap. Salty, creamy feta is a welcome accompaniment, as is a cold glass of wine—you can't beat Paleokerisio, a semi-sparkling orange.

NOTE: *The recipe makes 4 small galettes but is easily doubled if you're serving a larger group. Bake on two racks positioned in the upper and lower thirds of the oven and switch racks halfway through baking.*

1 Bring a medium saucepan of water to a boil over high heat. Add the salt (you want this water wildly salty, as the rice doesn't cook in it for long), stir in the rice, and cook until the grains are al dente, 6 to 8 minutes. Drain the rice in a sieve, rinse with cold water, then set aside to cool for 5 minutes.

2 While the rice cooks, place the spinach in a kitchen towel and squeeze over the sink to expel as much water as possible. Transfer the spinach to a medium bowl.

3 Stir in the rice, garlic, chickpeas, raisins, yogurt, oil, lemon zest, and lemon juice to the bowl of spinach. Season with more salt and pepper to taste. Refrigerate this mixture while rolling out the crust, or for up to 24 hours in an airtight container.

4 Preheat the oven to 375°F (190°C) with a rack positioned in the center. Line a sheet pan with parchment paper.

Recipe continues

**CRUST VARIATION
OPTION:** Whole Wheat
(page 39)

5 Roll out 4 dough rounds using the Tiny Method (page 36) and arrange evenly spaced on the lined sheet pan.

6 Scoop ½ cup (125 g) of the rice mixture into the center of each round and spread as needed for a 1½-inch (4 cm) border. Brush the border around the filling with some egg wash. Fold the edges of the crust over the filling toward the center, overlapping and pleating as desired. Repeat with the remaining 3 dough rounds (you may not use all of the filling—save it for a snack). Freeze the galettes on the sheet pan for 20 minutes.

7 Remove the galettes from the freezer. Brush more egg wash over the exposed crusts.

8 Bake until the crusts are deeply golden brown and the filling is starting to take on color, 40 to 50 minutes, rotating the sheet pan front to back halfway through. If any of the edges unfold during the first half of baking, you can use a butter knife to gently refold them when rotating the pan.

9 Remove the galettes from the oven and cool, uncovered, for 15 minutes or up to 2 hours.

10 Serve, topped with sliced or crumbled feta.

Leftovers can be stored in an airtight container in the refrigerator for 24 hours. Reheat on a sheet pan in a 350°F (180°C) oven until warmed through, about 10 minutes.

It's Not a Galette, But. . .

The spinach-rice mixture makes an excellent dish on its own: Heat 2 tablespoons olive oil in a nonstick or cast-iron skillet over medium-high heat. Press in the rice mixture and heat until the mixture is warmed through and the bottom is well crisped, 10 to 12 minutes. If you feel so inclined, after adding the rice to the pan, make a couple of holes in the rice with a wooden spoon and crack in eggs, then cover and cook over medium heat until the eggs are set to your liking.

CHOPPED MUSHROOM AND KIMCHI

Mushrooms are roughly 90 percent water, meaning that the best way to harness their earthy flavor is to cook out that excess liquid. In this case, the job is done via a take on classic duxelles: minced mushroom and onion sautéed until deeply fragrant and nearly dry. Fold in chopped kimchi to build on the mushrooms' umami, though you'll notice the fermented cabbage bakes off sweeter than when munched on straight from the jar. Don't skip a shower of razor-thinly sliced scallions just before devouring.

NOTES: *Clean mushrooms by wiping them with a damp towel; if they're super-dirty, rinse with water, wipe clean, and dry well.*

Use a food processor to make quick work of chopping the mushrooms and onion. Work in two or three batches to ensure the vegetables are very finely chopped but not pureed.

SERVES 4 TO 6

¼ cup (50 g) vegetable or olive oil

1½ pounds (680 g) white button, cremini, and/or stemmed shiitake mushrooms, very finely diced (about 7 cups)

1 medium yellow onion (5½ ounces/160 g), very finely diced (about 1¼ cups)

1 tablespoon soy sauce

1 heaping cup (200 g) drained, finely chopped cabbage kimchi

1 standard disk A Good Crust (page 27)

Egg wash: 1 large egg, beaten

3 scallions, trimmed and sliced very thinly on the bias

Toasted white or black sesame seeds, for serving

CRUST VARIATION OPTION: Whole Wheat (page 39)

SERVE WITH: Jammy eggs (page 194)

1 Heat 3 tablespoons (40 g) of the oil in a Dutch oven or large deep skillet over medium-high heat. Stir in the mushrooms and onion and cook, stirring occasionally, until the mushrooms have softened and their water has released and then cooked off, 10 to 15 minutes.

2 Reduce the heat to medium, stir in the soy sauce, and continue to cook, stirring often, until the mixture is sticky and nearly dry, another 8 to 10 minutes.

3 Meanwhile, set up a large bowl of ice and water for an ice bath.

Recipe continues

4 Remove the mushrooms from the heat, scrape into a medium bowl, and set in the ice bath. Let cool to room temperature, about 15 minutes.

5 Stir the kimchi into the mushroom mixture. If not baking the galette immediately, after 15 minutes, transfer to an airtight container and refrigerate for up to 2 days.

6 Preheat the oven to 425°F (220°C) with a rack positioned in the center. Line a sheet pan with parchment paper.

7 Roll the dough into a round and set it on the lined sheet pan using the Basic Method (page 34).

8 Spoon the mushroom mixture into the crust, leaving a 2-inch (5 cm) border. Fold the edges of the crust over the filling toward the center, overlapping and pleating as desired. Freeze the galette on the sheet pan for 10 minutes.

9 Remove the galette from the freezer and brush the egg wash over the exposed crust. Drizzle the remaining 1 tablespoon oil over the filling.

10 Bake until the crust is starting to turn golden, 12 to 15 minutes. Reduce the oven temperature to 375°F (190°C) and continue to bake until the filling has browned and the crust is deeply golden brown, another 40 to 50 minutes, rotating the sheet pan front to back halfway through.

11 Remove the galette from the oven and cool, uncovered, for 15 minutes or up to 8 hours.

12 Scatter the scallions over the galette and sprinkle with sesame seeds. Slice and serve.

Leftovers can be stored in an airtight container in the refrigerator for up to 2 days; if you don't mind wilting the scallions, reheat on a sheet pan in a 350°F (180°C) oven until warmed through, about 10 minutes.

RESOURCES

Depending on where you live and the season you're baking in, everything you need to make any galette in this book should be available at your local supermarket or kitchen supply store. Some highly specific ingredients and tools may require a trip to a specialty store; if there are none in your area, head online for dozens of retailers from which you can order. I've shared a few of my preferred brands in each category.

KITCHEN SUPPLIES

Bench and/or bowl scrapers
Ateco (atecousa.com)
Matfer Bourgeat (matferbourgeatusa.com)

Cast-iron skillet
Field Company (fieldcompany.com)
Lodge (lodgecastiron.com)

Chef's knife
Material Kitchen (materialkitchen.com)
Victorinox (victorinox.com)

Digital scale
Escali Primo Digital Food Scale (kitchensupply.com, homedepot.com)

Lightweight cotton kitchen towels
Zeppoli (walmart.com)
IKEA/Hildegun model (ikea.com)
Choice (webstaurantstore.com)

Offset spatula
Ateco (atecousa.com)

Pastry brush
Tezzorio (amazon.com)
Winco (wincous.com)

Petty/prep knife
Zwilling (zwilling.com)

Plastic wrap
Kirkland Stretch-Tite (costco.com)
W&P's Reusable Stretch Wrap (wandp.com, grove.co)

Sheet pans and sheet pan covers
Nordic Ware Naturals Aluminum Baker's Half Sheet (nordicware.com)

Vegetable peeler
Kitchpower (kitchpower.com)
Material Kitchen (materialkitchen.com)

SUPERMARKET BASICS

Most supermarkets should have the following items in stock. I'm sharing my favorite brands, but if one isn't available, buy what you can find.

All-purpose and whole wheat flours: King Arthur, Gold Medal

Buckwheat flour: Bob's Red Mill, Arrowhead Mills

Unsalted butter: Cabot, Kerrygold

Cocoa powder: Ghirardelli, Guittard

Cornmeal: Bob's Red Mill, Indian Head

Jams and preserves: Bonne Maman

Maraschino cherries: Luxardo and Fabbri are the best, but any store's offering will do (and will often be cheaper).

Spices (ground and whole): While supermarkets are likely to carry everything you need, some single-origin spices may need to be sourced at specialty markets/online—when in doubt, look for Diaspora Co. or Burlap & Barrel (and see some other brands called out below).

Tahini: Villa Jerada, Lebanon Valley

Vanilla extract: Heilala and Nielsen-Massey (high quality and quite expensive); McCormick pure vanilla extract (more affordable)

Za'atar: Z&Z, Canaan Palestine

SPECIALTY INGREDIENTS

Depending on where you live, some of these may be available at your local supermarket, but don't be disheartened if not. Visit small Italian, Middle Eastern, and Asian markets in your area, or look online for the best delivery options.

Calabrian chiles (crushed or chopped, in oil)
  Divina (divinamarket.com)
  Tutto Calabria (tuttocalabria.com)

Candied (glazed) orange peel
  Fratelli Sicilia (nuts.com, eataly.com)

Chili crisp
  Fly By Jing (flybyjing.com)
  Lao Gan Ma (laoganmausa.com)

Halva (or halawa)
  Al Wadi (sahadis.com)
  Hebel & Co (hebelco.com)

Harissa
  Mina (mina.co)
  Villa Jerada (villajerada.com)

Miso paste
  Marukome (hmart.com)
  Miso Master (wholefoodsmarket.com)

Orange blossom (or flower) water
  Al Wadi (sahadis.com)
  Nielsen-Massey (nielsenmassey.com)

Piment d'Espelette (or Espelette pepper)
  Biperduna (simplygourmand.com)
  Donostia Foods (donostiafoods.com)

Preserved lemon
  Casablanca Market (whole and puree/paste; casablancamarket.com)
  Mina (mina.co)
  Tara Kitchen (tarakitchen.com)
  Villa Jerada (villajerada.com)

Ras el hanout
  Rumi (rumispice.com)
  Spicewalla (spicewalla.com)

Rose water
  Al Wadi (sahadis.com)
  Nielsen-Massey (nielsenmassey.com)

Sumac
  Edy's Grocer (edysgrocer.com)
  Villa Jerada (villajerada.com)

Yuzu koshō
  Ocean Foods (umamimart.com)
  Youki (gohanmarket.com)

ACKNOWLEDGMENTS

I personally love reading cookbook acknowledgments, because it's incredible to see how many people it takes to make books like these. If this is the first time you read one, I hope it's not the last!

Thank you to my parents, Gail Barresse and Alan Firkser, who have let me make messes in their New Jersey kitchen for three decades (including one very big day of photographing this book). I can't possibly thank you properly in a couple of sentences, but know I'm able to do what I do because of your support.

To Kitty Cowles, my agent, for believing in me. I hope this is just the beginning of much great work we'll make together.

Thank you to my editor, Judy Pray, for your keen eye. I loved seeing my work get stronger every time you took a pass.

Madeline Firkser, thank you for listening to me spiral and then telling me all the ways I'm okay. We're so lucky to have each other.

Susan Goldman, my CAS: "Generous" isn't a big enough word to describe you, but thank you thank you thank you for everything you've done, and do, for me.

Eric Kim, Alexis deBoschnek, Emily Schostack: Thank you for letting me bounce idea after idea off you, for complaining with me about food media, for speaking my culinary language.

It was a gift to collaborate with such a deeply talented, in-sync, and, above all, kind creative team. Jessica Marx, thank you for your attention to detail, your world-building lighting, and your wealth of production advice (I love my new steamer). Julia Rose, thank you for creating the most beautiful scenes, for knowing exactly which platter to pick when I just wanted the yellow ones, for adjusting every fork. Thank you both for agreeing to my taking on the role of food stylist for the book, even though I've never been the food stylist on a book before—I think it worked out. Thank you for letting me adjust and futz and zhuzh in your areas of expertise to make each shot feel like "me." It was truly only after our shoot that this collection of words and food started to feel like a book. I'm so outrageously proud of these images.

To Megan Litt, for being my second pair of eyes and hands on the photo shoot. (And thank you again for your perfect countertop oven–sized sheet pan.) You are so good at your job and an absolute joy to be around.

To friends who gave up some of their time to hold galettes in the spotlight: Clara, Elizabeth, Eric, Julia, Robyn, Sam, and Sophia. I hope all your résumés now include "hand modeling" as a special skill.

I had so many incredible recipe testers on this project—thank you all for your time and insight. Thank you especially to Jessie Levin for giving your first test as much attention as your fourteenth.

Alison Roman: Thank you for taking a chance on working together back in 2019. You taught me so much, from how to pack Fresh Direct bags for shoots to using food coloring to dye my bowl scraper to styling food in a way that is beautiful but also "real." I'm a better cook and writer because of you.

Thank you Zoe Denenberg, Madeleine Preiss, Phoebe Fry, Kiley Nelson, Clara Hawn, Elizabeth Neibergall, Steve Riddle, Tara Holland, Melody Anderson, Sophie Haulman, and Julia Weinberg for the contributions you made to this book. Thank you Katherine Lewin for the "!". Thank you Shio Studio for your space, and especially your giant refrigerator and speed rack. Thank you to Cabot and Kerrygold for supplying (so much!) butter for our photo shoot and the recipe development process.

And finally to Ben Grund, who would always eat one more bite of galette if I asked (even when we were both so sick of them). Thank you for ordering me salad anyway when I said I was too full of pastry. Thank you for letting me fill our refrigerator with butter and carpet our floor with grocery bags. Thank you for telling me to take a break sometimes. I love living life with you.

INDEX

REBECCA FIRKSER is a Brooklyn-based writer and cook. Her recipes and writing have appeared in *Bon Appétit*, Food52, TASTE, Eater, and Epicurious, among others. She writes a newsletter, *Nickel & Dine*, celebrating budget-based recipes that are flavorful and exciting. The "k" comes before the "s" in her last name. For more, visit rebeccafirkser.com.